Assignments as Controversies

Approaching academic assignments as practical controversies, this book offers a novel approach to the study of digital literacy. Through in-depth accounts of assignment writing in college classrooms, Bhatt examines ways of understanding how students engage with digital media in curricular activities and how these give rise to new practices of information management and knowledge creation. He further considers what these new practices portend for a stronger theory of digital literacy in an age of informational abundance and ubiquitous connectivity.

Looking also at how institutional digital learning policies and strategies are applied in classrooms, and how students may embrace or avoid imposed technologies, this book offers an in-depth study of learner practices. It is through the comprehensive study of such practices that we can better understand the efficacy of technological investments in education, and the dynamic nature of digital literacy on the part of students charged with using those technologies.

Ibrar Bhatt is Lecturer in Education within the School of Social Sciences, Education, and Social Work at Queen's University Belfast, Northern Ireland.

Routledge Research in Literacy

Edited by David Barton, Lancaster University, UK

Assignments as Controversies

Digital Literacy and Writing in Classroom Practice

Ibrar Bhatt

Routledge
Taylor & Francis Group
LONDON AND NEW YORK

First published 2017 by Routledge

2 Park Square, Milton Park, Abingdon, Oxfordshire OX14 4RN
52 Vanderbilt Avenue, New York, NY 10017

Routledge is an imprint of the Taylor & Francis Group, an informa business

First issued in paperback 2018

Library of Congress Cataloguing-in-Publication Data
A catalog record for this book has been requested.

ISBN: 978-1-138-18545-6 (hbk)
ISBN: 978-0-367-19429-1 (pbk)

Typeset in Sabon
by Apex CoVantage, LLC

Contents

Preface

In this book I explore how equal access to digital technologies does not necessitate an equal experience of digital literacy. My interest in this topic grew out of my work as a teacher of Literacy and English as a Second Language around the inner-city areas of Leeds and Bradford, in the north of England. Whilst teaching newly arrived and unemployed migrants and refugees in a community centre, I noticed how my students would write, behave, and interact differently when they were using computers and phones. Some of this was outside of the class period, and some, troublingly at the time, was not. I began to think about what this means for Literacy, and what resources the students were drawing from as they connected with people online and behaved as core participants of digitally-mediated communities through buying and selling, arranging travel, and organising their lives; yet at the same time they remained very much marginalised in everyday society and of a 'low' Literacy level in the world of the classroom. I began to ponder how these other literacies have cultural histories that I had not experienced, that they belonged to communities of practice that I was not part of, and more importantly how the students leveraged those literacies for personal enhancement. I felt like I needed to better understand those literacies, even though they were a world apart from the kind of reading and writing the students were engaging in with me inside the classroom. This interest is what lead to this book.

The research for this book was planned and conducted between 2010 and 2014 at three college sites in West Yorkshire, in the north of England. The book represents a revision and expansion of my PhD research completed at the University of Leeds (UK), and I should like to thank a number of people for supporting me in its completion. These include: my PhD supervisors, James Simpson and Mike Baynham, for their guidance and support; my examiners, Simon Green and Mary Hamilton; and the college teachers and students who granted me access to their classrooms to carry out field work and data collection. I am also grateful to the following people for their insights and comments upon earlier drafts of sections: Mary Lea, Beth Cross, David Barton, Sharon McCulloch, Sadia Khan, and Peter Kalu. A special thanks also to the following people for various kinds of personal support: Khadija, Maryam, Zaynab, Nazneen. As well as Zahira, Imran, Elena, Khalid, Natalia, Maryam, and Betül.

I should acknowledge some of the other places in which aspects of this research have been written and spoken about. These include primarily my PhD thesis, and papers with the following journals: *Educational Media International* (Vol 49, 4), *Research in Learning Technology* (Vol 21, 4), *Language & Education* (Vol 29, 6), two annual conferences of the Society for Research into Higher Education (SRHE), and, more informally, the reflections in my personal blog.

I am also grateful to people in the following places for inviting me to present on this research and gain useful feedback: the University of Nicosia (Cyprus), The Literacy Research Centre (Lancaster University), the Digital University Network (SRHE), BURCH University Sarajevo (Bosnia & Herzegovina), the White Rose Doctoral Training Centre, the Open University, and the Centre for the Advancement of Research and Development in Educational Technology (CARDET, Cyprus). Finally, I should acknowledge the UK's Economic & Social Research Council (ESRC) for funding this research as a doctoral scholarship.

1 Introduction

Sites of Controversy

This book is about controversies. Specifically, it is about controversies within assignment writing in classrooms. It presents stories that offer plots that introduce a cast of 'actors'. Sometimes these actors have their own complex and awkward relationships. Through this book, I chart the plot of student writing through an investigation of practices and relationships. The *controversies* that I refer to in the title of the book emerge through the relationships between actors implicated in classroom activities and assignment writing. This book is not necessarily about how teachers teach, learners learn, or how these relate to the digital evolution of classrooms, though these things are related to its topic. It is about dissecting the plot to see how student work actually gets done in modern college classrooms.

With the research set in different college sites in the north of England, this book presents three uniquely different accounts of classroom writing. It is based on my study (Bhatt, 2014), which investigates the moment-by-moment practices that went into writing tasks as students sat at their desks getting on with the work set by their teacher. I explore the cultures of information and communications technologies (ICTs) within classrooms, how they relate to the tools immediately available to those involved in the assignments, interactions between actors both within and beyond the immediate context, and the rules and expectations governing those interactions and their outcomes.

What will follow are stories to show the way digital literacy actually 'happened' in three modern and digitally infused classroom spaces. Through an ethnographic approach, which was augmented by videographic methodologies, I present vignettes of sequential processes where we see not only the outcomes of established and commonplace literacy activities but also the disjunctures, impasses, and breakthroughs in practices of digital literacy. By shining a light on what worked and what was encouraged and inspired, as well as what did not work and what was hindered, avoided, and thwarted, I attempt to expose and discuss the tensions in the students' experiences of digital literacy and ultimately develop a critical understanding of digital literacy *policy* versus *actuality*.

The sociologist Erving Goffman in his essay "The Underlife of a Public Institution" (Goffman, 1961), enumerates the ways he observed patients in a secure mental health ward, sometimes manipulating institutional resources and facilities for their own purposes. Goffman collectively terms these practices as the "underlife" of the institution, and argues that they "represent the ways in which the individual stands apart from the role and the self that were taken for granted for him by the institution" (Goffman, 1961: 187). As a site of analysis, a modern college classroom is a curious and complex stage with its own rich and varied underlife practices. It is through these practices that students can develop autonomy and nurture relationships that are otherwise explicitly repressed in the institution.

Even with today's technological advancements, a classroom still appears as a sectioned-off physical space where a fixed number of students conduct standardised educational activities under the guidance of a designated person and often with a routinised mode of operation. Yet new digital media have altered the spatial and temporal dynamics of a conventional classroom and dislodged more traditional pedagogies. New digitised classrooms now have porous walls in which students' practices can traverse physical and virtual realms. These practises have changed the nature of learning and teaching in tremendous ways, and brought forth new actors that either did not previously exist or had no place in the more traditional classroom. A lot of this takes place beyond the sight of teachers, professors, college quality inspections, and the managerial directives of what a college deems as 'good practice'. I attempt to get at these elided practices, to see how they emerge through choices and dilemmas, and then theorise upon their involvement within curricular assignment tasks. It is through these practices that my focus emerges as the classroom as a site of 'controversy'.

This leads me to study acts of classroom writing from a cultural and social perspective, and to draw from a well-established tradition of research often referred to as the New Literacy Studies (or Literacy Studies). This approach to literacy, outlined in detail in the next chapter, brought a shift in the study of literacy—a shift which was heavily influenced by anthropology—and a need to refocus literacy inquiries away from psycholinguistic processes of a reader or writer and towards ethnographic methods to uncover the role of texts in communities and networks of practice. Context, therefore, is the starting point in Literacy Studies; this is the commitment that reading and writing are located as part of *social practices* and occur within culturally constructed instances or *literacy events* (see Heath, 1983). Within this book, I further discuss a prototypical notion of the literacy event and how, through pervasive digitality and connectivity, events such as course assignments are less situated in a given time and space. Rather, as I elaborate in a later chapter, they are deeply nested within other events in a multi-layered ecology of practice. A student may face a multitude of impasses and breakthroughs during assignment writing, and may have to work around difficulties in order to maintain an apparent coherence to the task. The same holds for a teacher issuing and helping with an assignment. What, therefore, emerges in the writing of an assignment is far from a predictable set of practices.

Why Study Assignments?

Assignments, as curricula genres, have been the subject of research in the field of rhetoric and composition, and writing across the curriculum (WAC). Researchers working in these fields (e.g. Bazerman & Russell, 1994; Bazerman, 2010) have, over the last few decades, investigated the multifaceted nature of how written language is taught, learned, and produced, and the broader social processes within which writing practices are embedded. Research in the field of student writing and genre (e.g. English, 2011) has also proven to be insightful for educational purposes—particularly in understanding students' lives outside of their colleges or schools, and how their lives can relate to writing pedagogies. However, this research has tended to focus on describing and analysing the structures and functions of genres, and how students can be instructed to produce them. My observation of assignment tasks as key literacy events complements this body of research.

'Assignments as controversies' explores digital literacy practices in the classroom experience of college students. Every day, and in classrooms everywhere, teachers give many kinds of assignment tasks to students. These can include anything from dissertations, short essays, and digital- and paper-based portfolios. Such tasks can be procedurally framed to acknowledge elements of new digital literacies. This can be through a kind of token gesturing, such as the requirement to word-process assignments, and submit work digitally. However, even assignment tasks which look decidedly digital in product and process often remain grounded in an educational system which valorises more traditional kinds of literacies. We get to see these by following an assignment writer's practices as they negotiate their task and deploy available resources: how they do—or do not—abide by the set procedural requirements of the task, how they must garner information, present their work, make arguments, submit, etc.

We can perhaps better understand these practices by viewing a student on a course as someone who is traversing a river. At certain points along the way, they become misdirected by the current or by periodically hitting rapids. At these points, the pace of activity speeds up, and things can get bumpy and uncertain. An assignment task at this moment has much converging upon it to bring a student back on track. In many ways, assignments hold a course together and much depends on them, with teachers using them to assess student progress and ascertain their grasp of a subject being studied. Assignment tasks, therefore, serve a vital pedagogic function and are events that can tell us a lot about how student literacies relate to learning.

Charles Bazerman's (1988) investigation of scientific writing fits well with this approach. Bazerman talked of writing as being an act contained within a historical context. A moment of writing is an encapsulated moment in time which follows a chronology of events leading up to it, but which also foretells its own future. Shaped by interactions between varying forces within those moments, the act of scientific writing, much like assignment writing, can take on new characteristics and evolve in future iterations and renditions. Bazerman argued that the expansion of the genre of the scientific article evolved to shape the enterprise of science altogether. In the same way, the practices through which assignment tasks are characterised and accomplished are bound up with different texts and a multitude of 'actors' which are situationally relevant to students' literacies: economic imperatives, managerial directives, quality assurance procedures, etc. Such actors can influence a particular and dominant conception of what an assignment task is, how it *should* be completed, and define the scope of the valorised literacies that it is designed to assess, thereby shaping the literacy moment and, importantly for composition theorists, the genre itself.

Where digital technology in the classroom has expanded not only learning spaces but also the nature of learning itself, genre becomes relevant once again. In her book *Everyday Genres: Writing Assignments across the Disciplines*, Mary Soliday (2011) argues that assignments are a traditional genre into which students attempt to shoehorn their practices of writing, but that they also remain "isolated from the social worlds that produce and sustain them" (Soliday, 2011: 84). The affordances of digital learning environments allow for a fluidity of practices and therefore the emergence of both deliberate and incidental *transcontextual* flows (discussed in Chapter 6 and Chapter 8). Given the transformative effects of digital learning spaces and new writing tools, the production of a genre may continue to remain a pedagogic goal but *how* it is produced needs to be attended to. A consequence for teachers and others interested in assignment and curriculum development is that digitality and connectivity open the door to new forms of writing across curricula.

WAC researcher Dan Melzer's (2009) analysis of the rhetorical features of 2,100 writing assignments across 400 undergraduate courses showed that enhanced writing skills through college programs can lead to better overall student performance in assignments. Yet movements to implement WAC courses in institutions of higher education and colleges have encountered significant resistance by administrators and faculty alike. In this book, I add to this debate by showing that assignment writing strategies can include practices which emerge through the wilful crossing of boundaries. These can be boundaries of time, place, and social sphere on the part of a student carrying out an assignment. There subsequently are a number of things at play in the writing of assignments, and each of these suggests a different point of interest and focus in this research. These include the student having to contend with the set procedures and discursive practices of an assignment, the need to synthesise and curate information across digital platforms and tools, and finally the creation of new content to accomplish the assigned task.

This focus of research inquiry becomes even more textually rich as complex digital actors become involved in the practices of assignment design, completion, and assessment. This is because academic content is but one aspect of assignment completion; situational practices are also shaped by wider enterprises such as policy goals which, in turn, shape a certain order in the day-to-day practices of a classroom (Hamilton, 2009). It is within this framing that in this book I focus on the *digital literacies* of assignment writing as part of the learning process and the role of these literacies within the regulatory frameworks of assessment and quality in education.

This focus leads me to view assignments as theoretical and practical controversies which require unpacking and exploring in order to better understand how digital literacies are played out in real assignment writing events. In my endeavour to investigate assignments in this research, I attend to the digital literacy practices which emerge during writing, and the kind of work that gets drawn into task completion. These are practices which give an assignment its character and enable its successful achievement for student, teacher, line manager, head of department, parents, and all actors directly or indirectly involved in an assignment's completion. I hope that through addressing course assignments in this way, as in flux and emerging from the practices of their moments, that we can better understand how such tasks are undertaken in programmes of study. Curricular assignments are, after all, evolving pedagogical forms. In-depth explorations of how they are written can tell us a lot about how we can improve them as tools of assessment.

With this in mind, and to set this book apart from other books which have explored either classroom digital literacies or curricular writing, I posed the following questions in my research:

What are the emerging digital literacy practices of learners as they work on writing assignments in a classroom setting?
How do these literacies relate to the learners' everyday literacies and habits with technology?
Are there any discrepancies between the way learners carry out their work and the requirements and expectations of their course and, more broadly, the college?

How This Research Was Done

As new literacies emerge from old, information, knowledge and meaning-making become redefined in the digital age, especially for what they contribute to the efficacy of learning and teaching. The nature of what we investigate as researchers then becomes as important, and uncertain, as the tools and methods of investigation themselves. Writing theorists who have made curricular assignments their object of inquiry (e.g. Mary Soliday and Charles Bazerman) have highlighted that assignment tasks are subject to the interpretations and negotiations within the complex social systems of classrooms and institutions. For this reason, I have found it useful to approach my study of assignment writing through a series of individualised case studies.

The study adopted a phased ethnographic approach in three different college sites—all situated in the north of England. The college sites have been renamed here in this book as Abbeydale (Chapter 3), Woodale (Chapter 4), and Northdale (Chapter 5). UK college contexts are complex and fascinating sites for the study of literacy, and I sought to build on prior work in this area (e.g. Ivanič *et al.*, 2009). However, much of the terminology specific to UK college contexts has been removed in this account to provide a wider and more international appeal to the book, except where it has been necessary to use a term that is specific to the English college system (e.g. the levels of courses), in which case a footnote explanation is provided.

The data collected from the three college sites eventually lead to a case study of a learner's assignment for a particular programme of study within each site. Key considerations in the selection of the college courses were that they had embedded vocational elements and that there were significant differences in the course-related activities of the learners. Particular attention was also paid to ensure that assignments in each setting differed by type, format, and style in order to capture a broader range of writing practices. The vocational element was important in order to gain insights into the kinds of digital literacy practices influenced by, and drawn from, the work experience of the students, and how their particular work-based practices may influence the practices of an assignment. Importantly, these practices could potentially emerge from, interact, or compete with other literacy practices during the writing of their assignments. The three courses selected on this basis were Certificate in Childcare (Chapter 3), Technology for Learning and Delivery (Chapter 4), and English for speakers of other languages (ESOL) and ICT (Chapter 5).

Each site was investigated in three phases. Phase 1 of data collection involved regular visits to the college sites and observations across a period of three to five months. This consisted of ethnographic observations of institutional culture and classroom activities. From this phase of data collection, I selected a student in each of the three sites whose assignment writing I would record and trace during class time as part of phase 2 of the data collection process. The students selected have been renamed in this book as Sara (Chapter 3), Anne (Chapter 4), and Paulo (Chapter 5). This second phase entailed using a videographic methodology which captured the entire process of on-screen composition. This was integrated with an embedded video and audio recording of the students' movements and verbalisations around the tasks at the time of writing. This provided me with a 'screen-in-screen' format of the recordings and therefore a rich, multimodal rendition and in situ monitoring of the assignment writing unfolding. I was able to see each student's on- and off-screen interactions (including discussions and gestures) and real-time interactions with the computer (typing, copy-pasting, browsing, etc.). I collected three videos to view, one for each case being explored, and meticulously transcribed segments as part of the analysis.[1]

After the video recordings of assignment-writing events were complete, I interviewed each student about their practices of digital literacy across home, work, and college. This represented phase 3 of the data collection process for this study. Following a participatory ethnographic approach, this part of the research design was enhanced by incorporating a Venn diagram task within a post-assignment interview. The Venn diagram task aimed at identifying and mapping practices of digital literacy and tools for personal, classroom, and work use, and the "boundary crossings" (Ivanič & Satchwell, 2007) among them. In the three student interviews, discussion centred on where and how, within the video recording of their assignment work, practices flowed across different spheres of life activity (work, home, etc.) and how practices initiated in one sphere of life became mobilised by them as resources within their classroom-based writing.

In addition to field notes made during initial observations, photographs taken of the college environment, and transcribed discussions with the student participants, video data became central to the "thick description" (Geertz, 1973) of the classroom practices investigated in the research. For example, by means of the video recordings, I was able to draw attention to the moment-by-moment digital literacy practices of assignment work. I was able to uncover not only how these practices emerged from established networks of actors during the class (i.e. learners doing what they should be) but also how, at times, other kinds of practices broke down these networks which together upheld a certain institutional culture (i.e. learners not doing what they should be).

Outline of This Book

Assignments as Controversies is divided into nine chapters across three main parts. Part I focuses on the background to the study, the literatures I have drawn from, and the theoretical resources which have shaped my research, including the fieldwork and analysis. Much of this discussion centres on conceptions of literacy and digital literacy, as well as my deployment of the theoretical tools of actor-network theory (ANT).

The chapters within Part II are accounts of the findings from the research. Chapters 3–5 are each qualitative accounts of Sara's, Anne's, and Paulo's assignments presented as vignettes. These are drawn from both my field notes and video logs of the recordings (see Bhatt, 2017), and augmented by an explanatory and analytic commentary. Venn diagrams from the interview component of the research are also presented and discussed with each case.

The chapters in Part III then turn more explicitly, and in more detail, to issues that were raised in Part II. Each chapter discusses a practical or theoretical topic from the research more extensively. Chapter 6 ("Buried in the Matryushkas") problematises the nested nature of literacy practices and the interconnectedness of literacy events. This sets the theoretical tone for Chapter 7 and Chapter 8. Chapter 7 focuses on the students' strategies in completing their assignments through managing and mobilising resources.

I present this idea as *curation*, and I connect its practice, as a latent form of digital literacy, to the goals of education and knowledge production. Chapter 8 highlights flows of new digital literacy practices within formal learning spaces. I define these flows as *irruption* and describe them as practices which originated from somewhere other than the classroom yet were mobilised, through actors, into the assignment event. To understand irruption, I argue, we have to look at how assignment writing becomes organised and systematised through various streams of practices.

In looking broadly at supporting theories, then specifically at practices, followed by a deeper look at the implications of those practices, this book makes the argument that digital literacy is not monolithic; it is dynamic. The dynamism and innovation contained within modern student digital literacies must be fully understood and evaluated in classrooms in order for changes in learning, literacy, and knowledge creation to be reflected fully in education.

Note

1 For detailed accounts of this method, see Bhatt and de Roock (2013), Bhatt *et al.* (2015), de Roock *et al.* (2015), and Bhatt (2017).

Part I

2 Literacy, Technology and Society

Perspectives on 'Literacy'

> English teenagers are most illiterate in the developed world.
>
> (*The Independent*, January 2016)

> Poor teen literacy levels linked to high screen time.
>
> (*Sydney Morning Herald*, February 2016)

> Teachers are having to work harder to find lessons that distract students from the digital mind swamp.
>
> (*Times Education Supplement*, February 2016)

Text, media, and information are more available and infiltrated into society today than at any time in history. Constant access to an abundance of online content at the click of a mouse or tap of a touch screen has radically reshaped how we socialise, inform ourselves of the world around us, and organise our lives. Yet despite the abundance of texts in our lives, the shocking headlines at the beginning of this chapter report what is perceived as a decline in literacy levels. They appear to harken to an imaginary of a previous time when things were better and literacy was imagined to have been done 'properly'.

What are the conditions that have made people perceive of literacy in this way? In getting at the answer, we may need to ask a few more questions such as the following: *What does it mean to be literate? Who benefits from this framing? How has widespread digitisation influenced this? What are the forces that sustain it in education, society at large, and the media?* These questions bring us to the debates discussed in this chapter, which begin by first discussing the nature of literacy. This is followed by a discussion of how literacy is associated with technologies and digital environments, and how these relate to the evolving nature of society. The chapter ends with a rationale for a way to better understand digital literacies through ongoing research which engages with the users of digital media, and which studies digital literacies as they unfold at the level of practice. Using this as a basis, we can attempt to uncover the role that digital literacies play in educational moments, such assignment writing, and the actors that lie beneath those moments.

Literacy as a Set of Skills

If the criteria to answer the aforementioned question, 'What does it mean to be literate?', are simply the abilities to read and write, then this assumes certain things: (i) that literacy is simply a matter of ability, or cognitive skills; (ii) that these skills are to be applied the same everywhere reading and writing are required; and (iii) that such abilities will likely be attained through an instructional process. This constitutes a 'functional' approach to literacy—one which focuses on the "basic skills" that people must possess in order to "fulfil their economic and social potential" (Holme, 2004: 12). A functional literacy perspective also entails that people will master the skills of literacy to different degrees (Holme, 2004: 17). A discussion of this position is necessary to begin with, and this begins by problematising the notion of literacy as exclusively a set of *skills* to be acquired.

The word 'skill' originates from an Old Norse word which means 'to separate'. In educational practice, skills can be considered as hierarchically represented, discrete, and systematised into ordered sub-components, or 'sub-skills'. Skills for any activity (e.g. word processing) are also thought to be attained through training and other instructional activities (see Curzon, 2004: 291–305). On this basis, the notion of literacy as a set of skills continues to hold a great deal of influence in educational practice and is often reinvigorated in recurring educational literacy policies. According to Barton (2007), in this approach,

> Literacy is seen as a psychological variable which can be measured and assessed. Skills are treated as things which people own or possess; some are *transferable skills*, some are not. Learning to read becomes a technical problem and the successful reader is a *skilled* reader. As a school-based definition of literacy, this view is very powerful, and it is one which spills over into the rest of society.
>
> (Barton, 2007: 11)

Barton further argues that a skills perspective points to literacy as relating to individually possessed "neutral techniques" which remain the same "across all situations" (Barton, 2007: 163). This view of literacy remains widespread across many parts of society and shapes everyday perceptions about what it means to be literate, including media narratives around literacy—as suggested in the headlines at the top of this chapter. This view is also at the heart of many policy formulations regarding what to do about a 'lack' of literacy.

In a wholly skills-based view, literacy is used in the singular and refers to a decontextualised and disembodied set of skills which are taught by prescription and considered measurable and unproblematically 'transferable' from one domain to another. This chapter begins with a critique of this discourse, which has often resulted in teachers having to cast aside their learners' vernacular literacies of home, community, and work as potential resources, and give prominence to curricular literacy practices in the daily workings of a college classroom (Smith, 2005). Regarding this disjuncture, Street (1997: 48) claims, "If literacy is seen as simply a universal technical skill, the same everywhere, then the particular form being taught in school [and by extension college] gets to be treated as the only kind".

Street (1984) further conceptualises this traditional approach as an 'autonomous model' of literacy. Simply put, the autonomous model holds that literacy is a technical skill, autonomous from the social acts in which it occurs, neutral in that it has no relation to the power struggles of its contexts, and characteristic of the psychology of the individual reader/writer. He juxtaposes this with his 'ideological model' of literacy in which literacy is "always embedded in socially constructed epistemological principles" (Street, 2009: 29). In this framing, literacy practices are always tied to a social order and value system, and hence to engage with literacy becomes a form of critical social inquiry.

This forms the basis of the 'social practice' approach to literacy. This approach complemented earlier views of literacy which focussed on more individualistic-cognitive or psychological approaches to language. It also critiqued their failings in how they neglect to take into account social phenomena, value-laden features of literacy, and literacy activities beyond classrooms and colleges. What counts as literacy in a social practice perspective, therefore, depends on the social institutions in which literacy is embedded, the processes through which it is acquired, and the practices through which it is enacted. It is, therefore, a matter of literac*ies* rather than a singularly conceived literac*y*. This study of college assignment writing draws from this social practice view of literacy, germane to which is a focus on what people actually do with texts and how they are used to get things done, and invites careful and ethnographic attention to social acts of meaning ascribed to them (Baynham, 1995; Barton, 2007).

Cognitive Consequences

Debates examining the development of literacy and its social and cognitive effects are by no means new; the issue has been debated for centuries. Plato's Phaedrus records Socrates' objection to the practice of writing, stating that it would erode memory and cognitive functions (Jowett, 2008). A more contemporary example of this ancient debate, of the alleged link between literacy and cognitive abilities, emerged through the empirical investigations of

A. R. Luria (Luria, 1976) at the behest of Lev Vygotsky in the early 1930s. Luria's investigations were among peasant communities in Uzbekistan and rooted in experimental psychology. He held that the material conditions of culture, and the way that social groups live out their realities, ultimately shape cognitive structures. Luria set out to test these ideas by conducting a series of experiments with two groups of peasants. The first of these groups had never been to school and had only experienced an agrarian lifestyle. The second was an 'educated' group who had undergone a basic literacy education. Luria's results revealed that schooled peasants were able to engage in reasoning and conclusions beyond first-hand experience. The unschooled peasants, however, were unwilling to infer novel conclusions based on propositions about which they lacked personal experience, thereby not engaging with the logic of a situation outside of their immediate experiential context.

Luria's research pointed to a mechanistic relationship between literacy and cognitive development and became the frame for subsequent thinking and research on the supposed consequences of literacy. This view appears to have converged with a school of thought which held that literacy acquisition brings with it certain cognitive consequences (Goody & Watt, 1968; Goody, 1977; Olson, 1977; Havelock, 1982; Ong, 1982). This tradition came to be known as the *literacy hypothesis*, and much of it developed through the work of the Toronto School of Communication. Proponents of this range of perspectives differed slightly in their conception, but generally held that literacy, and its acquisition process, is an engine of radical cognitive change. The development and diffusion of literacy was said to cause a restructuring of a literate person's psychological life.

Some theorists (e.g. Havelock, 1963; Goody & Watt, 1968) claimed that Western civilisation itself was born as a direct result of the introduction of the phonetic writing system in Ancient Greece and the subsequent literate cultures that flourished. These literacy theorists argued that the very acquisition of textual literacy skills is responsible for the development of profound cultural and psychological consequences (e.g. abstract thought and reasoning). This resonated with the mediational framework of Luria.

A criticism of Luria's conclusions (and, by extension, the literacy hypothesis view) was that it left open the question of whether or not it was literacy per se or education (that is, the social process of formal schooling) that influenced performance among the 'literates' and 'semi-literates' of his study. These, and similar arguments, form the basis of a line of research inquiries which sought to take account of the wider social, material, and historical factors in better understanding how literacy is understood and practiced by people in day-to-day situations.

Scribner and Cole's Counter-Thesis

Amongst the critiques of the literacy hypothesis in its strong version was the one advanced by Sylvia Scribner (a developmental psychologist) and

Michael Cole (a cultural psychologist) in their landmark book *The Psychology of Literacy*. Their research (Scribner & Cole, 1981) set out to discover whether it is literacy or formal schooling that affects mental functioning, and if it is possible to distinguish between the effects of forms of literacy used for different functions in the life of an individual or a community. They used the Vai-speaking community in Liberia, a society where literacy was not *necessarily* associated with formal schooling, as the base for this investigation. For the Vai, English is spoken and written in school, and their indigenous language is adopted outside school. The latter is not a schooled literacy; it is used for social conventions, such as letter writing, and uses a non-Roman script. The Vai is also a Muslim society, so the Koran is visibly and audibly part of everyday life, with many able to recite it in Arabic. The Vai, therefore, have one, two, and, in some cases, three of the aforementioned forms of literacy. Scribner and Cole state their approach to their research, and their emphasis on 'practice', as follows:

> Instead of focusing exclusively on the technology of a writing system and its reputed consequences ("alphabet literacy fosters abstraction" for example) we approach literacy as a set of socially organized practices which make use of a symbol system and a technology for producing and disseminating it. Literacy is not simply knowing how to read and write a particular script but applying this knowledge for specific purposes in specific contexts of use.
>
> (Scribner & Cole, 1981: 236)

In psychological tests, Vai literates who were formally schooled in English performed better than other groups. Scribner and Cole (1981) thereby concluded that literacy, independent of formal schooling, does not result in the generalised cognitive effects assumed by Luria and theorists of the literacy hypothesis. However, even among the schooled literates, those who had been out of school for a longer period were noticeably weaker on the tests than those who had more recently left school. The counter-thesis proposed by Scribner and Cole states that the educational process of *schooling* is what leads to the cognitive and wider effects discussed earlier, and not learning to read and write per se, as Havelock, Goody, Watt, and others had claimed. The counter-thesis is one primarily about *causality*; the question of whether literacy (*sensu* the skills of reading and writing) is a sufficient cause of particular cognitive effects (higher order reasoning, etc.).

There were also other findings in Scribner and Cole's research. The literates, both formally schooled and otherwise, were better than non-literates at understanding and explaining the formal features of written and spoken language. Whilst this shows us that formally schooled literates are better able to use and describe language in certain ways, subjects who were literate in Vai only (and so not formally schooled) showed similar abilities when talking about the correct language of letter writing in Vai. This work was therefore seminal, as it shows us that literacy is associated with, and realised through, 'social practices' rather than a formally schooled understanding of correct language.

This also suggests that formal schooling leads to rather specific abilities that are valued and rewarded in institutional and wider societal contexts but which, in fact, constitute only *one* form of literacy among other possible 'literacies' that people in a given society may be socialised into. Scribner and Cole (1981) concluded,

> Literacy is not simply knowing how to read and write a particular script, but applying this knowledge for specific purposes in specific contexts of use. The nature of these practices, including of course their technological aspects, will determine the kind of skills ('consequences') associated with literacy.
>
> (Scribner & Cole, 1981: 236)

Acknowledgement of the Social

Researchers have since moved away from the view that literacy has direct 'consequences' in terms of superior cognitive skills, to a view which recognises that there are different purposes and ways in which literacy is used. Gee (2008) comments as follows:

> The Scribner and Cole research clearly indicates that what matters is not "literacy" as some decontextualised "ability" to write or read, but the social practices into which people are apprenticed as part of a social group.
>
> (Gee, 2008: 80)

Brian Street further critiques the literacy hypothesis of Goody, Ong, Havelock, etc. He achieves this critique by characterising its conception as an 'autonomous' model of literacy—one which sees literacy as an autonomous engine of social and cultural change. He argues that these literacy theorists failed to theorise the conceptual basis for meaning-making in the societies which lack a written culture (Street, 1984). In making this critique, he contrasts the 'autonomous' model of literacy with an 'ideological' model, outlined in more depth later in this chapter. Through this framing, Street (1984; 1995) builds on the work of Scribner, Cole, and others, and illustrates how literacy is historically and culturally situated and attached to the values, practices, and politics of particular communities. Literacy, therefore, is defined and upheld by specific communities (or sectors of communities) who may have a stake in maintaining a particular notion of 'literacy' and a particular set of values, practices, and politics commensurate with that notion: one which legitimises a certain distribution of power, resources, and socioeconomic structures.

These arguments have brought researchers to an acknowledgement of the social and how experimental approaches which assume literacy to be quantified, measured, and assessed independently of context are quite simply not enough to understand language phenomena and literacy in particular. In the wake of Scribner and Cole's (1981) seminal study are a host of ethnographic studies which have sought to explore the real-life embeddedness of reading and writing in people's lives. Two notable studies that are worth discussing because of their relevance to this research are those of Scollon and Scollon (1981), and Heath (1983).

The Scollons studied discourse practices and how they relate to identity shifts of the Athabaskan community in Alaska. According to the Scollons, in Athabaskan culture, in order to engage in the displays of knowledge required in essayist prose, Athabaskans would need to know the audience and be in a position of dominance, yet this relationship is obscured in essayist prose, as both author and reader are fictionalised and the text decontextualised. The Scollons proved that essay-text literacy represents a challenge to some cultural and ethnic identities, and acquiring this literacy is not simply about learning a new skill but about being enculturated into certain ways of being and knowing.

Heath's (1983) focus was on the way children in poor black and white working-class neighbourhoods in the US acquire language and literacy in the process of becoming socialised into the norms and values of their communities. There were two concerns: 1) the implications of this socialisation for the acquisition of other literacies and 2) how literacy nurtured in preschool years reflects the social practices associated with literacy and ways of knowing in the family and community.

Neither of the children's socialisation experiences within their respective communities prepared them for the norms and practices of mainstream educational literacy. Both working-class communities tended to value an experiential, orally mediated, empirically based, and non-analytical view of learning not indicative to school-based practices. These children lacked the foundational components of a particular type of literacy which would likely get them far in academic contexts.

A 'New' Literacy Studies

This brings us to the notion that literacy is always associated with some sort of social activities; they are socially situated and practised within various communicative networks. This social stance on Literacy Studies has theoretical foundations in several disciplines, including anthropology. Social perspectives on literacy practices take context as their starting point, and indeed, main focus of inquiry. Baynham and Prinsloo (2009) in their introduction to *The Future of Literacy Studies* outline this approach to Literacy Studies, sometimes referred to as the 'New Literacy Studies', although it is no longer 'new' and henceforth discussed as *Literacy Studies*.

According to them, this approach draws upon two previous generations of works in the area. Amongst them are the works of Heath (1983), discussed earlier, and Street (1984), which shifted the focus of literacy research wider and into society. Literacy Studies drew inspiration from a range of 'social turn' movements of the latter half of the 20th century (Gee, 2000), and is based on the view that literacy practices only make sense when they are studied through a sociocultural lens.

Anthropologist Brian Street's research in Iranian villages also demonstrated the "multiple literacies" (Street, 1984) evident in the different contexts and domains of his study. The varying forms literacy can take, depending on different contexts and purposes, are key in a social practice perspective on literacy. Street conducted his ethnographic research in the 1970s in north-east Iranian villages on the border with Afghanistan. He discovered various literacy activities undertaken on a daily basis by people who were described as 'illiterate' by literacy campaigners in the region at the time. These literacies, however, were not the ones taught and valorised in educational settings, they remained marginalised to the everyday social and informal realms of society. Additionally, there was literacy practiced in Koranic schools in the region, which also contained a certain amount of complexity and sophistication in how it was performed, handled, and passed on. Again, this literacy was not deemed as 'proper' literacy from a dominant and normative perspective. This lead Street to reflect that if the complex variations in literacy evident in a small locale were decidedly shaped by outside agencies (e.g. state education, literacy projects), then this might also be the case elsewhere. Street's subsequent proposed new understanding stimulates literacy researchers to be sensitive to the richness, variety, and complexity of everyday literacy, especially amongst those people conventionally classified as 'illiterate'. Such classifications are based on a version of literacy; they are therefore 'ideological' and part of the plurality of literacies in the fabric of everyday society.

Given this multiplicity, Street works from the "ideological model" of literacy (Street, 1984). According to this model, literacy is not a purely technical or cognitive achievement which is characteristic of the psychology of the individual reader/writer, but one which is "always embedded in socially constructed epistemological principles" (Street, 2009: 29). Hence, to engage with literacy is in itself a "social act" (Street, 2009) and one must consider the multitude of communicative contexts in which literacy occurs. This is contrasted with his notion of the more traditional "autonomous" model, which views literacy as a discrete set of skills that can be taught in isolation regardless of context. The autonomous model is germane to the notion of 'functional literacy' and the cognitive consequences notion of literacy outlined earlier.

The wider ideological model sees literacy as shaped by a sociocultural environment and tied directly to a social order. It is by no means a neutral activity, as those who are in socio-political control determine who has access to certain literacies through educational and policy decisions. Since literacy practices are so ideologically charged, then any claims for the consequences of literacy, according to Street, "will not so easily be disguised as universal truths" (Street, 1984: 29).

This forms the basis of the critique of earlier views of literacy which assumed more cognitive or psychological approaches to language, failing to take into account social phenomena and what is beyond the text, the person, and the classroom. In this way, the ideological model of literacy *subsumes* the autonomous model in the way that Street has conceptualised them. What counts as literacy, therefore, depends on the social institutions in which it is embedded, the processes through which it is acquired, and the practices through which it is enacted. This is in contrast to literacy being understood solely as an autonomous technology that everyone has the same chance of attaining or acquiring. Furthermore, he asserts that even the autonomous model (of Goody, Havelock, Watts, etc.) is actually ideological at its core in that it "disguises the cultural and ideological assumptions that underpin it and that can then be presented as though they are neutral and universal" (Street & Leftsein, 2007: 41).

For scholars of Literacy Studies, therefore, literacy is primarily a socio-political construct rather than a purely linguistic one, and the following tenets of Barton and Hamilton (2000) help encapsulate literacy in these terms:

- **Literacy is best understood as a set of social practices; these can be inferred from events which are mediated by written texts.**
- **There are different literacies associated with different domains of life.**
- **Literacy practices are patterned by social institutions and power relationships, and some literacies are more dominant, visible and influential than others.**
- **Literacy practices are purposeful and embedded in broader social goals and cultural practices.**
- **Literacy is historically situated.**
- **Literacy practices change and new ones are frequently acquired though processes of informal learning and sense making.**

(Barton & Hamilton, 2000: 8)

Literacy Events and Practices

To describe and investigate the literacies of particular contexts, literacy researchers employ a construct known as 'literacy practices', evidence of which can be derived from Heath's (1983) notion of a 'literacy event' and subsequently developed in a number of studies (Scribner & Cole, 1981; Heath, 1983; Street, 1984; 1993; 2009). This study of assignment writing is underpinned by a conceptualisation of the assignment as a literacy event, which is performed into being through a diverse array of literacy practices. Beginning with literacy events, as situational encounters with texts, allows this study to complement and subsume—but not replace—a traditional 'skill-set' notion of literacy, outlined in previous sections. Prinsloo and Baynham (2008) clarify as follows:

> Typically researchers have observed or recorded particular literacy events at their site of research and then tried to understand the wider discursive framings and social practices that cause such events to take their particular form and shape. "Literacy events" have thus provided the empirical units of analysis in the study of literacy, whereas "literacy practices" have provided an analytical frame that includes both activities and conceptualisations of reading and writing.
>
> (Prinsloo & Baynham, 2008: 3–4)

In analysis, researchers begin with a literacy event as an empirical occasion involving interaction around a written text from which they then infer both abstract and empirical literacy practices. These can be attained through other sources in addition to recording and documentation of literacy events, such as participant interviews. Notably, a key and empirical definition of 'practice' is that of Scribner and Cole's (1981: 236), who defined it as "a recurrent, goal-directed sequence of activities using a particular technology and particular systems of knowledge". Thus it is quite action oriented. Another related but more abstract construct of practice as "a combination of action and reflection" (Baynham & Prinsloo, 2009: 5) owes its origins, via the work of Bourdieu, to Karl Marx's theses on Feuerbach:

> The principal defect of all materialism up to now—including that of Feuerbach—is that the external object, reality, the sensible world is grasped only in the form of an object or an intuition; but not as concrete human activity, as practice, in a subjective way.
>
> (Bourdieu, 1977: vi)

Literacy practices, then, involve the literacy activity, related texts, ideologies, and patterns of behaviour surrounding those texts, attitudes, and values that inform them, and ultimately the broader ethnographic detail (Tusting *et al.*, 2000: 213). In the exploration of literacy practices there necessitates the need to ask *who* is doing *what*, *to whom*, *why*, *for whom*, *where*, *when*, and, moreover, *who benefits*? What becomes central in the capture and analysis of literacy events is the "configuration of action, talk and text" (Prinsloo & Baynham, 2008: 4). Schieffelin and Gilmore (1986) justify this ethnographic approach to the study of literacy as follows:

> Literacy, viewed as a cultural phenomenon that interacts with certain social processes, is best studied by adopting an ethnographic perspective. By ethnographic we mean descriptions that take into account the perspectives of members of a social group, including the beliefs and values that underlie and organize their activities and utterances. An

> ethnographic perspective allows the researcher to find out the meaning of events for those who are involved in them. This entails investigating the contexts of the uses of literacy, the meanings of literacy, and the forms of literate communication as it is organized and plays a role in organizing particular social interactions.
>
> (Schieffelin & Gilmore, 1986: viii).

Later in this chapter, I will outline a notion of practice to complement and enrich the one described earlier. This is a notion which draws from the sociology of actor-network theory and a sociomaterial understanding. Taken together, these perspectives on practice can yield fruitful and interesting insights in a study of college students' assignment writing and their digital literacies. But first, it is important to further discuss some of the work in Literacy Studies which has investigated college learning.

Literacies in College Learning

A defining characteristic of the UK college sector is its incredibly diverse student population. College learners do not fit any specific profile, and courses consist of people of various ages undergoing second-chance school courses, university-level programmes, and a plethora of vocational courses. Consequently, a learner in a college can be on a programme of study anywhere from the most basic 'pre-entry'[1] level up to university degree or even master's level.

UK colleges have therefore been the subject of various literacy research inquiries, including a notable study by Ivanič *et al.* (2009) which investigated the literacy practices of students across their social and college contexts. The project, entitled the Literacies for Learning in Further Education (LfLFE) project, explored the disjuncture between the literacy demands of college courses and students' preferences in outside-college contexts. Ivanič *et al.* (2009) contend that taking account of students' vernacular literacy practices can improve learning in college and that these practices ought to be acknowledged in educational decisions and curricula design. The LfLFE project, therefore, highlights the abundance of "unmapped literacies" that have the potential to be "brought into play" for life in the classroom (Nash *et al.*, 2008: 6). As participation in colleges widens, and student constituencies diversify, the disconnects between personal and curricular literacies is one of key importance for literacy researchers and college educators. These literacy disconnects can be more of a problem for learners in vocational courses over academic ones. Childcare students, for example, need to address a wide variety of audiences through their various literacy activities. These can include literacy activities in college lessons and assessments, and more work-oriented things such as logbooks for colleagues and parents, and different kinds of reports (Smith *et al.*, 2008).

In their research, Ivanič *et al.* (2009) show that college students engaged in an abundance of complex and sophisticated literacy practices outside of their formal spheres of learning, yet these very students were deemed by their colleges as having 'problems' with literacy. The purpose of the project, therefore, was to locate, recognise, and better understand these *other* literacies and then work with teachers to develop pedagogic approaches which harness them as resources in curricular work. The insights and findings gained from this project are directly relevant to the subject of this book. This is because the conclusions of Ivanič *et al.* lead us to question the widespread assumption that a simple 'lack' of literacy holds learners back. The richness and complexity of students' everyday literacy practices can—and should—be a source of effective teaching and learning.

The research reported on in this book builds on the work of the LfLFE project by examining how learners tap into and mobilise certain kinds of resources during assignment writing, and in so doing make their own unsolicited alterations of a normative classroom literacy culture. In the LfLFE project, the researchers discovered a clear abundance of digital literacy practices in students' everyday lives, alongside a prevalence of paper-based literacy practices in their college courses (see Satchwell *et al.*, 2013). A natural next step to this kind of research is one which examines how students make these mobilisations *themselves* through using digital media, rather than through pedagogic interventions.

Further Developments in Literacy Studies

Theoretical perspectives in literacy research have diversified and grown since the foundational counter-hypothesis of Scribner and Cole, and the anthropological works of Heath and Street. This is acknowledged explicitly by Baynham and Prinsloo (2001) who describe Literacy Studies as a

> network of inter-related theoretical interests, differently emphasised and inflected in the work of different researchers, but nevertheless permitting the continuation of an ongoing theoretical conversation.
>
> (Baynham & Prinsloo, 2001: 84)

Examples of such ongoing theoretical conversations taking place within the broad remit of Literacy Studies can include Brandt and Clinton's (2002) critique of *localism*, Clarke's (2002) case for ANT approaches to literacy research, Kell's (2006) notion of *transcontextuality*, and Gourlay and Oliver's (2013) call for *sociomaterial* perspectives to better understand day-to-day practices of digital literacy.

This study of student assignment writing contributes to these lines of thought and builds upon their endeavours to push forwards the tradition of Literacy Studies. As the tradition attempts to apply its ethnographic and critical lenses to the study of digital literacy, we may have to generate widening conceptions of how literacy events and practices are understood empirically and conceptually in digitally mediated environments. And we may also have to develop the ethnographic toolkit that we use to research literacy, with new kinds of data to be collected and new kinds of research questions posed (Bhatt *et al.*, 2015; Bhatt, 2017). Next, I provide the foundation for such an analysis and explore developments in Literacy Studies alongside the notion of sociomateriality as an ontology to illuminate the entanglements of texts, people, and technologies in the contexts of assignment writing.

In their position paper in the *Journal of Literacy Research*, Brandt and Clinton (2002) argue that the ethnographic *localism* of Literacy Studies can fail to take into account wider and distant agencies which impinge on the situational context of a literacy event. Technologically, local forms of communication are entwined with global networks and systems, and it becomes imperative to conceptualise and describe literacy with sensitivity to these:

> If reading and writing are means by which people reach—and are reached by—other contexts, then more is going on locally than just local practice.
> (Brandt & Clinton, 2002: 338)

Connected to this are the material dimensions to literacy and how material agencies are integrated within literacy practices. Classroom digital literacies are shaped by ICT learning policies, funding directives, software scripts, personal and/or institutional devices, friends who are online and available, chat applications, and Internet connections, etc. The relations between these actors is not stable, and they rely on various elements working together collectively to hold a moment of digital literacy together. In this respect, the complexity of technological apparatuses is often ignored in a social practice conception of literacy.

Building on some of the points raised by Brandt and Clinton, Clarke (2002; 2008) advances a case for using ANT in her research of government policies and strategies on adult literacy and numeracy. Drawing on Latour, and echoing Brandt and Clinton, she claims that ANT sensibilities stimulate researchers to pay closer attention to the "far more disparate and often discordant array of entities" at play in ethnographic sites (Clarke, 2008: 157). She outlines how through these theoretical sensibilities, literacy researchers are able to uncover the configuration of actors that stabilise established ways of 'doing' literacy.

Another, similar, approach was adopted by Hamilton (2001; 2009; 2011) in her analysis of the International Adult Literacy Survey. To Hamilton, through using ANT as a theoretical resource, the material artefacts of documents maintained a certain structuring agency and lead to "certain kinds of knowing" (Hamilton, 2001: 178). Those who may have a stake in maintaining certain kinds of literacies define and uphold them, and this will include a particular set of values, practices, and social order commensurate with that notion.

However, in each of these cases, the researchers focussed on the generalised structuring agency of policy artefacts and not on how the forces shape and give rise to certain types of literacy unfolding at the level of practice in a given scenario (such as an assignment). To some extent, this is an issue of magnification. Gourlay and Oliver's (2013) work, by drawing on elements of posthuman theory (cf. Hayles, 1999), takes us closer to the actual 'doing' of day-to-day practices with texts (both print and digital). Their study is set in a university campus and explores the situated and emergent nature of students' daily practices with digital media. Through focus groups and multimodal journaling, they found that students' engagement with digital devices occurred across a range of time/space realms and often beyond the archetypal 'university' spaces (lecture rooms, libraries, Virtual Learning Environment (VLE), etc.). Highlighting areas for the possible improvement of institutional provision, their work also reveals the "resilience, initiative, and ingenuity with which students work around problems by enrolling other people, places, and things in their practices" (Gourlay & Oliver, 2013: 94). Building on Gourlay and Oliver's theoretical contentions, sociomateriality is a notion central to this study of assignment writing and further discussed later in this chapter.

Also drawing on Brandt and Clinton, Cathy Kell's (2006; 2009) work in South Africa similarly explores literacy as it is enacted across space and time. Presented as a transcontextual approach, she interrogates the notions of 'locality' and 'localism' in literacy ethnographies and the limitations of framing ethnographic accounts of literacy practices as bounded within an ostensible site or context. To do so is problematic to Kell (2006), as literacy events spill over across various social spaces and time frames. She argues, "Modes and media of communication carry meanings within the streams and flows that make up the texture of the contemporary world" (Kell, 2006: 147). In her transcontextual analysis of literacy practices, Kell (2009) draws on the theorist Bruno Latour to argue that literacy practices have a life beyond an essentialised notion of an 'event' and that researchers ought to move "beyond the single instance" (Kell, 2009: 86) to witness their trajectories.

As the theoretical space develops, and as the field of Literacy Studies attempts to apply its ethnographic framing and critical lenses to literacy in digital environments, widening conceptions of literacy events and practices become necessary. As new and disparately located actors such as algorithms, software engineers, and portable devices become entrenched in the new digital sociality, much more is taking place in a single situated practice of literacy than previously envisaged. Existing theory may help situate research within an existing scholarly conversation, but in order to build upon and transcend prior work and help build and grow the body of knowledge, pragmatist philosopher William James asserts,

> Theory thus become instruments . . . We don't lie back upon them, we move forward, and, on occasion, make nature over again by their aid.
> *(James, 1907: 46)*

Perspectives on 'Digital' Literacy

In this section, I explore some of the recent literature on 'digital literacy' and relate this to the constructs of literacy practices, literacy events, and sociomateriality. As has already been discussed, the concept of 'literacy' is contested, malleable, and entwined with cultural and political discourses. Contributions to the scholarly conversation on digital literacy similarly bring different foci and perspectives to an understanding of literacy in digital environments. The following sections survey some of these main contentions in this area which, when considered together, form a grounding to how I have investigated assignment writing.

Literacies and the Digital

Over the last two decades, there has been an escalation in use of the prefix 'digital' in educational research, reflecting the wide-ranging impacts digital media have had across the entire spectrum of educational activity. Digitisation has influenced everything from the day-to-day practicalities of learning and teaching to the now prevalent institution-wide ICT administrations. Mandatory courseware management systems such as Moodle are now commonplace, as are the use of digital platforms for departmental and professional communities (e.g. Twitter and Facebook for networking). Theorisations around these changes have brought such notions as the 'digital university' (e.g. Goodfellow & Lea, 2013), the 'digital divide' (e.g. Norris, 2001), and the 'digital scholar' (e.g. Weller, 2011). In each of these fashionable and rhetorical usages of the term 'digital', the implied significance has been the discrete importance of new media to whatever issue, context, or subject is being problematised.

Given its use against the term 'literacy', the concept of 'digital literacy' becomes difficult to pin down, with shifts in definitions and applications, encapsulating a range of trans- and interdisciplinary research agendas (Gee, 2010). Terminologies have evolved, from an early vision of 'digital literacy' (Gilster, 1997), to 'electronic literacy' (Warschauer, 1999), then 'silicon literacy' (Snyder, 2002), followed by 'twenty-first century literacy' (The New Media Consortium, 2005), and a related concept of 'media-literacy' (Buckingham, 2003).

The advent of Web 2.0 technologies, at around the turn of the millennium, brought with it an emergence of scholarly interest in 'digital literacies' and a re-emergence of the term pertaining to the skill set required to operate and exploit Web 2.0 environments effectively. The kinds of digital literacies emerging in Web 2.0 environments have been broken down by some into such skills as 'remix literacy' (Lessig, 2008), 'attention literacy' (Rheingold, 2010), 'network literacy' (Pegrum, 2010), 'mobile literacy' (Parry, 2011), and 'web literacy' (Belshaw, 2014) etc. Each of these concepts has set out to problematise, in different but overlapping ways, the multifaceted relationship between literacy and digital media. Each of these aforementioned types of 'literacy' relates to a suite of skills required to engage with digital technologies effectively in the post-industrial economy, whether they are about locating resources, communicating ideas, or creating content.

This has brought us to a more recent conceptualisation and a broad consensual return of the term 'digital literacy' (e.g. Bawden, 2008; Chase & Laufenberg, 2011), but one which still hearkens back to early theoretical formulations of its meaning which focus solely on a person's skills and competencies related to the requirements of ICT use (c.f. Gilster, 1997). This is a digital literacy that relates to a technical and procedural mind-set, or palette of cognitive skills, that allows one to solve problems and perform effectively in digital environments. Through this framing, digital literacy is often perceived as the requirement—in a digital environment—of being able to function effectively and utilise digital platforms, devices, and communications systems. This perspective is often reflected in policy discourses and its adoption often results in initiatives to 'upskill' and 'train' staff and students in educational institutions in how to develop more digital literacy. It is, therefore, this juxtaposition of the somewhat technicist conception of 'literacy' as a popular metaphor for 'competency' which has endured.

Related to the field of Literacy Studies, there has emerged a field of study which has focussed its attention on the study of 'new literacies' (see Coiro *et al.*, 2008; Lankshear & Knobel, 2011). As with Literacy Studies, the study of new literacies applies ethnographic approaches to studying and conceptualising literacy, and seeks to go beyond the competencies of the individual in understanding the cultural logics of the new literacies of digital media environments. It focuses on the myriad ways of meaning-making in digital environments, how these shape and give rise to new ways of being and knowing, and new kinds of social relations and communities.

This aspect is salient, especially when it comes to the literacies drawn into assignment work and other assessed tasks in education. Were it that the evaluation of literacy were singular, then 'new literacies' or a reductive and technicist notion of 'digital literacy' might have remained solely a matter of inquiry within the field of computer sciences, leaving out the complexities of wider experience, social environments, and value systems. However, the assessment of literacy is not a singular matter of pass/fail or literate/illiterate any more than literacy is a matter of text void of meaning. Assignment tasks, as outlined in the previous chapter, are bound up within different discourses and interests (economic, managerial, etc.). This means that it is not only learners who are concerned with their results. Understanding the literacies of assignment tasks against the new literacies of a dynamic and multifaceted learning environment, with its new and powerful digital actors, becomes essential. In this vein, and following a broadening of the conceptualisation of digital and new literacies, there has been a wave of studies exploring how people use the connectivity of cyberspace to further their personal, social, and educational goals.

Other research endeavours which have focussed on a more expansive notion of 'digital literacies' (note the plural) include Martin and Grudziecki (2007), Bawden (2008), and Gillen and Barton (2010). These studies have sought to uncover the complex social, cultural, and technical practices emerging through literacy in digital environments. These investigations and critiques take us beyond Gilster's (1997) early vision of 'digital literacy' (note the singular) as simply a set of information management skills and the competencies involved in operating digital media generally. Lankshear and Knobel's (2008) pluralisation of the term echoes earlier visions of an expanded notion of 'literacies' (c.f. Barton and Hamilton, Scribner and Cole, Street, etc.) that takes us beyond the competencies of an individual. Their conceptualisation of 'digital literacies', also defined later in this chapter, encompasses the enculturations that relate to the myriad of meaning-making practices evoked across different digital environments.

A complex and nuanced picture of digital literacies comes to light through the work of Beetham *et al.* (2009), who investigated 44 cases of learning and teaching practice in UK colleges and universities. Their study reveals different conceptualisations of literacy across different practice-communities within and across institutions as they develop frameworks to respond to the various digital literacy agendas that the communities are subjected to. A distinction, therefore, is drawn between 'academic skills', 'information literacies', and 'communication and collaboration skills', with each conceptualised somewhat differently based on the requirements of a practice-community. This is in contrast to Lankshear and Knobel's all-encompassing term 'digital literacies' to describe all such practices which are "mediated by texts that are produced, received, distributed, exchanged, etc., via digital codification" (Lankshear and Knobel, 2008: 5) and "digital enculturation" (p. 7).

Gillen (2014) further advances a perspective on digital literacies which is founded in the sociocultural and ethnographic commitments of Literacy Studies. Gillen views digital literacies as existing through dynamic and entwined relationships between their actualisation in practices and their broader mediating contexts—that is, their tools of use, cultural norms, historical patterns of use and understandings, etc. This theoretical perspective, for Gillen, is combined with a commitment to ethnography consistent with established practices in the Literacy Studies tradition, which she then applies as a "virtual literacy ethnography" methodology (Gillen, 2009). Her data draw on chat logs, the project wiki and group forum, and show that the young people's participation in the virtual world is an intensely literate activity, contrary to an overly dichotomised view of 'new' literacies and more valorised established ones.

In an earlier work, Gillen and Barton (2010) offer a broad definition of digital literacies: "the constantly changing practices through which people make traceable meanings using digital technologies" (Gillen & Barton, 2010: 9). This definition, they argue, allows the specificities of digital literacy practices to be explored whilst retaining sensitivity and attention to broader social processes, thereby ensuring a continuity to the body of work in Literacy Studies. In this vein, they contend,

> A social practice view of digital literacy possesses continuities with a social practice view of literacy in general. This is one which starts from what people do, the meanings they ascribe to their activities and the ways they use reading and writing in their broadest senses to achieve their purposes.
>
> (Gillen & Barton, 2010: 9)

Further and more recent critiques of digital literacy models and frameworks have emerged from researchers who have also applied the ethnographic framing of Literacy Studies to digital environments. These include Gourlay *et al.* (2014), who argue that much recent rhetorical usage of the term digital literacy/literacies promotes competency-based agendas which reflect and promote the interests of institutional and organisational imperatives. They present a framing of the issues around digital literacies which highlights "the situated, political, day-to-day 'doing' and 'being' involved in digitally mediated engagement with texts" (Gourlay *et al.*, 2014). They further argue that without such a framing, educators can acquiesce to a strongly normative perspective on academic practice detached from the life-world of the student. Echoing this position, Gillen (2014) claims,

> Diversity of experience and the consequent inevitability of variation in understandings, values and dispositions are a strong obstacle in the path of those who think it possible to adopt any standardised, stand-alone perspectives on digital literacies and impose them on people with equal effects.
>
> (Gillen, 2014: 10)

Such expanding and unresolved definitions and conceptualisations of digital literacy/literacies have led to what Chase and Laufenberg (2011) refer to as its "inherent squishiness" (p. 535), with evolving and emerging technologies to shape both what digital literacies represents *and* how we go about examining them. Literacy Studies certainly provides a useful critique frame through its reconceptualisation of digital literacies from a disembodied skill set to embodied social practice, but in so doing, echoing Brandt and

Clinton's warning, it may have de-emphasised the problem of *materiality*. This aspect is further explored later in this chapter, after I revisit the idea of the *literacy event* in the following section.

Returning to the Literacy Event

Literacy events, as mentioned previously, are the central empirical occasions where literacy has a role. Far from being isolated instances of reading and/or writing, literacy events form part of highly contextualised encounters, such as religious rituals (Besnier, 1995) and bedtime stories (Heath, 1982). As a unit of analysis, they yield snapshots of the social and cultural order in which literacy activities are institutionally and organisationally mediated (Prinsloo & Baynham, 2008), yet also remain intimately tied to material culture (Brandt & Clinton, 2002).

In this research, I begin with cases of literacy events as the empirical activities around the production of assignments, which college learners must complete as part of their assessed work. Success in programmes of study depends on learners being able to negotiate and manage a variety of digital literacy practices commensurate with the literacy demands of their course and, more broadly, the college. The notion of 'event' as conceptualised by Heath (and developed by others) forms a useful heuristic lens from which to explore such assignment tasks. Doing so can expose the wide-ranging and protean practices that constitute classroom writing and how institutional inequalities and relations of power are all inscribed in situational encounters within a particular setting. This analytical approach allows for a deeper observation of practices and their contextual richness than through analysing people's digital literacy as a set of competencies and a wholesale exploration of practices alone. However, considering the literacy event as a unit of analysis, as I have in this research, throws up a possible set of ambiguities. What, for example, does a literacy event look like? How is it captured in its entirety? In a world saturated by digital text, does it exist in a hermetic here and now?

In focusing on classroom-based literacy events, this study is building on a research tradition within the Literacy Studies paradigm which initially turned researchers' attention away from pedagogic domains, as literacy began to be seen as not just confined to a school or college environment. As such, Literacy Studies turned its attention to the vernacular practices of people in their everyday lives in an endeavour to capture the literacies of people in everyday contexts. However, it is important to remember that the problems experienced in the 'everyday sphere' entail a need to *return* to the pedagogic sphere in order to complete the process of "fine tuning literacy for learning" (Ivanič, 2009: 109). This study attempts to conceptualise the multi-layered interface between social life and the classroom with respect to digital literacies. As Ivanič (2009) recommends, echoing Baynham (2004), research should move from the classroom to the everyday in order to move—with great improvements—back to the classroom again, thus proposing that much can be gained by "bringing the lens of literacy studies [back] to bear on learning and teaching" (Ivanič, 2009: 101).

Effective evaluation of literacy events in digital environments should also be productively grounded in a suitable theory and sociological method which relates the agency of technologies and artefacts to practices of literacy and how they are enacted over apparent time/space parameters. ANT furnishes social theory of this kind, and the following sections outline how I have drawn upon its palette of theoretical resources in this book. This will be presented first by a discussion of 'sociomateriality' as a theoretical sensibility and ontology, followed by how ANT-inflected approaches can be applied in this study of classroom writing.

Sociomateriality

Bruno Latour (2004: 227), in an essay on the entangled relations between nature and culture, argues against a priori divisions of 'social' and 'material' elements by asking readers to envisage a battlefield with soldiers:

> [A]ccount for the dynamic of a battle by imagining, first, a group of soldiers and officers stark naked; second, a heap of paraphernalia—tanks, paperwork, uniforms—and then claim that "of course there exists some (dialectical) relation between the two".
>
> [T]here exists no relation whatsoever between the material and the social world, because it is the division that is first of all a complete artefact. To abandon the division is not to "relate" the heap of naked soldiers with the heap of material stuff, it is to rethink the whole assemblage from top to bottom and from beginning to end.
>
> (Latour, 2004: 227)

All practices emerge from entanglements between people and things. During the writing of assignments, an array of non-human actors, such as software platforms, search algorithms, policies on digital literacy, lesson plans, social networking sites, and good practice directives, are inescapable in students' literacy practices. In fact, in moments where literacy practices occur, these actors are best understood as acquiring their characteristics through their interpenetration with the human participants of the literacy event.

More generally, material artefacts are part of our cultural inheritance and also embedded within our cognition (Hutchins, 1995; Hayles, 2012). This means, as Orlikowski (2007: 1437) contends, "there is no social that is not also material, and no material that is not also social". Literacy, therefore, is never separate from its technology. Sociomateriality can be seen as a performative kind of realism that takes account of this through a relational (or performative) ontology. Sociomateriality is therefore about re-evaluating, re-interpreting, and re-conceptualising the vitality of matter and material in practices, and how these entanglements themselves perform new worlds. The material vitality of digital literacy needs to be examined as part of the new social world which emerges from it.

Research following a sociomaterial approach challenges the deeply taken-for-granted assumption that technology and activity should be conceptualised as discrete, and advances a view that there is an inherent inseparability between the material (the technical) and the human in all activities, including literacy. Whilst sociomaterial themes emerge in slightly different ways across different theoretical spaces, including cultural-historical activity theory, spatiality theory, and complexity theory, it is most notable in ANT (see Fenwick *et al.*, 2011 for a detailed discussion). Sociomaterial accounts highlight the political importance of human and non-human agencies in the doing of literacy through their entanglement in practices, which together form broader social processes.

Edwards and Fenwick (2014) make a case for the utility of sociomaterial theory in making educational and social critique. Through an assemblage framing, they posit several critique-related questions that are relevant to researchers employing sociomateriality, particularly in educational research:

1 *How do material practices mobilise particular agencies?*
2 *What materials have authority and why (and, on what does their authority rest, within and outside particular systems of practice)?*
3 *How and why do certain combinations of things come together, and what particular effects do they perform?*
4 *Of what are the collectivities and collective actions made? At what sites, through what practices, and by which actors?*
5 *How is that which becomes included or excluded from collectivities determined?*

(Edwards & Fenwick, 2014: 12–18)

Through highlighting the political importance and agentive potential of human and non-human agencies in practices of literacy, sociomateriality helps us to more effectively study and understand digital literacies and the hybridised, multi-layered, and tensional configurations of practices. Researching digital literacies requires tracing the choreography of the sociomaterial practices which emerge when digital media are used for literacy activities, as they occur entangled in an array of fleeting networks and associations. This is evidently more pronounced with the connectivity of cyberspace, where digital literacy practices are characterised by much more immediacy and hyperconnectivity (Edwards & Usher, 2008). Sociomaterial approaches have the potential to uncover complexities of how digital literacies are enacted in assignments, as students' digital literacy practices are increasingly knit together with actors not always easily visible (e.g. algorithms, platforms, software) and break through the boundaries of different worlds (not just worldviews). These actors are complex entanglements in their own right. They both shape, and are shaped by, people's engagement with them. It, therefore, becomes important to attend to these new kinds of entanglements theoretically and methodologically. As Waltz (2006) persuasively contends:

> The disregard for material actors, the objectification of these actors and the overdetermination of them preclude more careful theoretical and empirical inquiry into the ways in which the persons and technologies are involved with one another in the construction of the social.
> (Waltz, 2006: 58)

Our current digitally ubiquitous landscape necessitates a theoretical inquiry into the nature of the consequences of technologies on literate practice, and vice versa, and to bring this to bear on literacy inquiries more generally. Our interactions with cyberspace are therefore neither wholly socially nor technologically determined. Petersen (2007) clarifies,

> Technological determinism argues that the internet changes everyday life as 24-hour access to the internet makes it a constant intruder which can disturb the private sphere of our lives and change the nature of this sphere sometimes against our own will. Social determinism would view technology as being neutral, as just another tool for the human will.
> (Petersen, 2007: 82)

This indicates a symmetry across social and material actors in relational activities and any entity which 'acts' is an 'actor' (or 'actant'), regardless of is figuration. Much research on e-learning merely provides a descriptive account of what machines are good at and what they soon will be good at. As properties and affordances of technology are in themselves the results of relational effects, tracing these effects—and the literacy practices which instantiate them—can help us theorise how things get to be the way they are and how we can change them. Since it is through the different sociomaterial assemblages that ways of 'being' and 'doing' literacy are realised, the extensive body of work inspired by ANT approaches provides a useful set of techniques to both think about and practically explore digital literacies, and the sociomaterial assemblages in which they can emerge.

Actor Network Theory

ANT's theoretical lens has been used increasingly by social scientists (e.g. Callon, 1986; Law & Hassard, 1999; Latour, 2005), researchers in education (e.g. Fenwick & Edwards, 2012; Rowan & Bigum, 2012), and literacy researchers (e.g. Clarke, 2002; Hamilton, 2011). Although there is no precise moment when ANT became a distinct approach to social theory, it has drawn on an intellectual backstory encompassing a range of ideas influenced by post-structuralism. Post-structuralism itself is hard to define, except as anything other than a rejection of structuralist thinking—that the whole of human experience is based on a series of underlying structures that give meaning to the world. In 1976, Foucault tried to sum up some of the central concerns of the post-structuralist movement. He argued,

> For the last ten or fifteen years, the immense and proliferating criticizability of things, institutions, practices, and discourses; a sort of general feeling that the ground was crumbling beneath our feet, especially in places where it seemed most familiar, most solid, and closest to us, to our bodies, to our everyday gestures. But alongside this crumbling and the astonishing efficacy of discontinuous, particular, and local critiques, the facts were also revealing something . . . beneath this whole thematic, through it and even within it, we have seen what might be called the insurrection of subjugated knowledges.
>
> (Foucault *et al.*, 2003: 6–7)

This revolutionary appeal, 'the insurrection of subjugated knowledges', has real-life analogues. Following the 1968 riots in Paris, worldwide escalations of social conflicts, and overall disenchantment with bureaucratic elites there came a stark reassessment of widely held Western political and ideological belief systems. Post-structuralists argued that a drastic realignment in how we thought about our world, and how we derived meaning from it, was necessary before we could begin to adjust to that changing world. Post-structuralism, therefore, became any means to deny grand meta-narratives and truths.

An innate concern of post-structuralism is between binary oppositions and an anti-essentialist stance. To understand any object and its implicit meanings, we must not only understand the object but also contributions to the object's creation. Foucault's influence on the development of ANT is substantiated by Matthewman (2013), who links Foucault's theorising of technology, power, and industrial development of the West with later lines of thought in ANT. This is well exemplified in the following argument by Foucault on the relational nature of power when looked at next to Latour's statement immediately afterwards:

> Power must be analysed as something which circulates, or rather as something which only functions in the form of a chain. It is never localized here or there, never in anybody's hands, never appropriated as a commodity or piece of wealth. Power is employed and exercised through a net-like organization.
>
> (Foucault & Gordon, 1980: 98)

That power is an effect of a 'net-like' organisation is closely connected to Latour's conception of power as "not a property of any one of those elements but of a chain [of human and non-human actors]" (Latour, 1991: 110).

It is precisely within these notions of anti-binarism and 'net-like' spatial and temporal structures, which were a dominant part of the French post-structural intellectual tradition, where we can see ANT's backstory emerging. In this vein, ANT is also closely connected to Deleuze and Guattari's (1987; 2004) analytic metaphor of the 'rhizome' to conceptualise the world and its spatial and temporal structures, discussed later in this section.

ANT eventually grew to become a family of theoretical resources which were inspired by—and derived from—post-structuralist ideas mentioned earlier and *ethnomethodology*, and mostly developed through studies of science, technology, and society. ANT conceptualises social phenomena as occurring through a messy configuration of networks in which actions are contingent upon a shifting set of actants and that activities such as learning are not solely psychological, nor are they entirely social, but that they are generated through the relational activities of sociomaterial networks or assemblages. Such ideas, especially that of 'assemblage', are very similar to Deleuze and Guattari's (1987; 2004) analytic metaphor of the 'rhizome' to conceptualise the world and its spatial and temporal structures. A rhizome, in the Deleuzian sense, is a plant with a centred root-and-stem structure. Searching for a theory to counter and supplant the hierarchical and binary thinking of the 19th century, Deleuze and Guattari advanced the notion of the rhizome structure as an antithesis to the tree structure (as advanced by structuralism) and is therefore characterised by actors' heterogeneity, multiplicity, flow, and fluidity. According to Deleuze and Guattari (2004),

> Unlike trees or their roots, the rhizome connects any point to any other point, and its traits are not necessarily linked to traits of the same nature . . . The rhizome is . . . composed not of units but of dimensions, or rather directions in motion. It has neither beginning nor end, but always in a middle (*milieu*) from which it grows and which it overspills . . . (it) operates by variation, expansion, conquest, capture, offshoot . . . it has multiple entryways and its own lines of flight.
>
> (Deleuze & Guattari, 2004: 23)

The rhizome metaphor connects closely with tenets of ANT, its intellectual successor project, by conceptualising 'assemblages' (a word shared by both traditions) as having no beginning and no end, but ceaseless in their connections. With ANT's injunction to follow actors and their connections, and a focus on the mundane practices that build realities, it developed as a powerful method for analysing scientific and technological knowledge building in contrast to pure Deleuzian philosophy (Law, 2009).

Distinctively, ANT does away with ontological distinctions and dualisms such as micro/macro, human/material, and agency/structure through an injunction to "follow the actors themselves" (Latour, 2005: 227), or better still to "trace the associations" (Latour, 2005: 207), thereby producing accounts of networked relations in practice. This has resulted in ANT as a set of theoretical resources that are notoriously difficult to encapsulate or define. Law (1999) sums up ANT's attack on dualisms in the following words:

> Truth and falsehood. Large and small. Agency and structure. Human and non-human. Before and after. Knowledge and power. Context and content. Materiality and sociality. Activity and passivity . . . all of these divides have been rubbished in work undertaken in the name of actor-network theory.
>
> (Law, 1999: 3)

Some have differentiated between 'classic-ANT' (Callon & Latour, 1981; Callon, 1986; Latour & Woolgar, 1986; Latour, 1987), which gave us the all-embracing heterogeneous *network* metaphor, and 'after-ANT', which develops this into the notion of a network as a *spatial* and *fluid* imaginary (Law & Hassard, 1999). In the latter formulation, what is *next to*, *above*, and *between* actors in an event is not defined or accounted for by metric distance or three-dimensionality, but seen in terms of actors' fluid patterns of relation. Actors in networks, therefore, produce and sustain their own *spatialities*. For example, through the various activities carried out through it, a computer in a classroom can facilitate writing activities, be a community builder, maintain friendships, be a symbol of the college's prestige and investment in technology by being photographed in glossy marketing material, and a visible investment to satisfy quality assurance, etc. So for Latour, no phenomenon is confined to one context, one discipline, or one way of thinking; he writes, for instance,

> The smallest AIDS virus takes you from sex to the unconscious, then to Africa, tissue cultures, DNA and San Francisco, but the analysts, thinkers, journalists and decision-makers will slice the delicate network traced by the virus for you into tidy compartments where you will find only science, only economy, only social phenomena, only sentiment, only sex.
>
> (Latour, 1993: 2–3)

Events, and their related phenomena, take place in such a fluid network where 'space' is not hermetically conceived of as 'classroom space' and 'social space', but as a conglomeration of actors that are only real insofar as they have some sort of effect on something else. Actors are defined by their relations and are not always loyal to the script set for them by humans. Latour's fictional account of the failed technology of Aramis (Latour, 1996) is a useful way to understand how a technology can be 'disobedient' or 'disloyal' to the interests of humans. A technology, Latour argues, does not fail (or act disobediently) because of an actor's inherent failing, but rather because of a multitude of actors' failures to sustain interdependence and compromise (p. 101). In the case of Aramis (a personal rapid transit system in Paris), Latour further argues that it failed as a system not because of any one particular actor, but rather because the actors as a whole failed to negotiate and adapt accordingly.

Going back to the classrooms in this study, and the writing tasks that took place within them, such events and their constituent literacy practices can be seen as emerging in actor networks, with movements and flows of digital literacy practices in different *strata* of people's lives, and emerging through technologies that are sometimes used for purposes disloyal to their designers' intentions. Following Edwards (2009), here I deliberately use the geological term 'strata' over 'context', as literacy events are not bound by institutional structures; they are "scrumpled" (Edwards *et al.*, 2009a) with other events and always juxtaposed in cross-network relations. In this respect, rather than separating entities, all contexts, including classrooms, are fluid and created through the agentive work of actors who are not always in situ. Instead, they consist of "continuous paths that lead from the local to the global" (Latour, 1993: 117) and are mixed with cross-network practices occurring within and through them.

Recent ANT and Ontology

More recent ANT-inflected studies have taken an 'ontological turn' (van Heur *et al.*, 2013) in the study of phenomena, and they take the view that through the diversity of sociomaterial assemblages, a multiplicity of realities are subsequently enacted. These studies draw from a perspective on ANT which holds that there are no independently existing realities except that they materialise and attain different qualities through their particular relations and configurations over space and time. Realities can, therefore, be 'collateral' (Law, 2012) and 'multiple' (Mol, 2002), rather than singular or coherent. I will return in more detail to Mol's and Law's conceptions shortly, but for now, it is important to emphasise that from this perspective, realities are inseparable from—and assembled by—the practices which emerge at a scene of interest. This relates to a 'performativity of practice' (Law, 2012: 161) and means we have to carefully attend to the ecology of practices (their contestations, impasses, breakthroughs, etc.) to see how they perform what would otherwise be seen as a priori realities such as lessons, assignments, and meetings. If an actor is seen not as an autonomous entity that pre-exists its relations, but as existing only through its relations, then a classroom *itself* is performed through sociomaterial practices, through such actors as its four walls and campus plans. This is a relationist philosophy.

In this sense, *performance* is about enacting "different versions of the 'real', of which there is no original, but only such different versions" (Sørensen, 2010: 16). If a particular version is more dominant or preferred, then we need to explore the sociomaterial relations which render it so. An assemblage framing renders performance "an involved process [between actors] rather than a single act" (p. 16), and therefore the *sine qua non* of a sociomaterial assemblage. What is 'behind the scenes' is also deemed as part of the performance as much as the 'front stage' in the Goffmanian sense (Goffman, 1990), as the forces and agencies which render some realities to be elided and less visible (or even totally hidden) are the result of assemblage activity and of equal interest.

In her innovative and seminal "ethnography of disease", Mol (2002) explores performativity in the diverse sociomaterial practices through which multiple versions of a disease (atherosclerosis) are enacted. Tracing the coordination and trajectory of the practices reveals how the disease was enacted in different parts of a Dutch hospital: the consulting room, the outpatient clinic, in radiology, the operating theatre, etc. In each of these locations, a different version of atherosclerosis was produced, and it is by following the different practices, including such things as the patient's pain upon taking steps, that the single atherosclerosis actually became multiple, and enacted—or assembled—by a multitude of coordinated sociomaterial practices. This is the basis of, what she dubs, a 'praxiographic' approach. An approach which "allows and requires one to take objects and events of all kinds into consideration when trying to understand the world" (Mol, 2002: 158). She argues that, "no phenomenon can be ignored on the grounds that it belongs to another discipline" (Mol, 2002). The operative word here is 'practice', taking us beyond the traditional notion of 'ethnography'. Mol further argues that using this method "we learn that in different sites, different atheroscleroses are enacted" (Mol, 2002: 119, note the plural). Every performance thereby creates, or re-enacts, its own world. Mol's coinage is meant to stimulate researchers to focus not just on human actors of social order, and their stories, but practices with and between human and non-human actors.

Another, related, perspective on the 'performativity of practice' that is relevant to the way a digital literacy event is conceptualised in this research is John Law's notion of 'collateral realities' (Law, 2012). This is the idea that realities are only ostensibly coherent and stable, and are actually held together—sometimes quite precariously—by fractal and disparate practices. These practices sometimes hail from different spatial and temporal locations and with different goals and realities attached to them, but have a role to play in the scene of analytic interest. These forces then produce an ostensible unity and singularity of an event, and through an exploration of their practices, we can see where and how powerful actors do their work. As some realities 'tell' others what to do and push them out of the way, and how and why this happens is dubbed 'ontological politics' (Mol, 1999).

Using some of Mol's methods, by tracing the coordination of practices, we can see how they can cross, circulate, block, and break through the boundaries of other competing worlds (not just worldviews) in a given event, as well as the ontological politics which can ensue. The writing of an assignment is a heavily political act with importance attached at every level of its completion. The various realities it manifests are each performed by a choreography of literacy practices around it. Following Mol's decidedly practice-oriented approach, Law further instructs sociologists to attend to the choreography of practices, even if in so doing we are lead beyond the site of interest. He provides a useful set of techniques to achieve this:

> First attend to *practices*. Look to see what is being done. In particular, attend empirically to *how* it is being *done*: how the relations are being assembled and ordered to produce objects, subjects and appropriate locations. Second, wash away the assumption that there is a reality out there beyond practice that is independent, definite, singular, coherent, and prior to that practice. Ask, instead, how it is that such a world is done in practice, and how it manages to hold steady. Third, ask how this process works to *delete* the way in which this sense of a definite exterior world is being done, to wash away the practices and turn representations into windows on the world. Four, remember that wherever you look whether this is a meeting hall, a talk, a laboratory, or a survey, there is *no escape from practice*. It is practices all the way down, contested or otherwise. Five, look for the gaps, the aporias and the tensions between the practices and their realities—for if you go looking for *differences* you will discover them.
>
> (Law, 2012: 171)

What is made clear through an examination of the various levels of practice involved in using digital media to inform a piece of work (such as an assignment), is that the number of networks engaged becomes enormous and, as Law writes, "Once we turn up the magnification we quickly find that there isn't an independent, prior, definite, singular and coherent real out there upon which the various reports of reality are based" (Law, 2009: 12). Therefore, what digital literacy is purported to be, in policies, frameworks, and other actors, may not correlate with the actual practices of students writing assignments, especially as they employ a range of personal and institutional digital media to support their work. Research which attends to these very practices with a suitable theoretical explanatory programme is therefore necessary. The philosophical underpinnings of this approach to sociology, according to Law, lie in Deleuze's work on the philosopher and mathematician Gottfried Wilhelm Leibniz:

> Every portion of matter can be thought of as a garden full of plants, or as a pond full of fish. But every branch of the plant, every part of the animal, and every drop of its vital fluids, is another such garden, or another such pond.
>
> (von Leibniz *et al.*, 1998: 277)

This philosophical sensibility suggests that every entity is a composite form with external relations, and an internal network of worlds within worlds. Entire worlds lie within the minutiae of practices performed in a phenomena of interest, through a kind of Baroque complexity (Kwa, 2002). This forces us to look 'down' at the fractal and inter-relational elements in motion in an event, rather than to look 'up' from a homogenous and essentialist abstraction of it (Hillier, 2007). Law draws us to the analogy of the Mobius band to further explain this, which folds and twists such that the inside and the outside are part of the same band worn on the wrist.

Applying the 'performativity of practice' (Law, 2012: 161) means we have to carefully attend to the ecology of practices to see how sociomaterial relations are assembled and realities, such as lessons and assignments are done. In other words, an assemblage of competing and disparate practices holds the cultural order of a literacy event together. This is a 'performative' conceptualisation of digital literacies: that digital literacy practices perform the reality of the classroom, the assignment, the game play, or whatever it is that the students are doing with devices. According to Gourlay and Oliver (2013), this perspective is a useful expansion to the view of literacy as an embodied 'social practice' (c.f. Barton and Hamilton, Scribner and Cole, Street, etc.) already discussed.

Computers in Classrooms

Building on the earlier discussion, we can view digital technologies that are available and utilised in classrooms as opening up possibilities for the reconfiguration of the space-time geometries of literacy events. The distributive nature of the practices of digital spaces forces us to problematise the reconfiguration of a learning and teaching 'context' as we have traditionally understood it to be (Edwards & Usher, 2008; Edwards *et al.*, 2009b). Petersen's (2007) work is relevant in addressing this question: He suggests that online environments create "a weakening of the usual structure of everyday life differentiated into different zones of work, study and recreation" (p. 86), thereby leading to a restructuring of everyday life and activities. For example, a group of writers editing the same document simultaneously using a cloud-based file management platform, and a student checking their course emails and VLE updates can do so through smartphone applications and at any time of the day or night. In both of these cases, users can potentially conflate their mundane uses of digital tools with their curricular or work activities. It is, therefore, in the tracing of the networks in which these practices occur that we are able to identify the ways in which 'digital' literacy is achieved practically.

The Re-Organisation of Relationships

Enthusiasts, protagonists, and theorists of the interdisciplinary fields of educational technology[2] and technology-enhanced learning (e.g. Salmon, 2004; Vrasidas & Glass, 2005; Bonk & Graham, 2006) have all investigated how rapid advancements in technologies and connectivity have revolutionised the way students learn. Added to this has been a booming interest in research and practice with educational technologies in classrooms, and how new technological dynamics are said to displace classic pedagogies. Reviewing the literature from this body of work is beyond the scope of this book, but most of this research has been about critiquing educational practice and learning efficacy. My concern in this book is the role that digital literacies play in educational moments such assignment writing and how digital literacy practices lie beneath these moments.

The mass installation of ICTs in classrooms often overshadow other developments which need to occur alongside them. Take, for example, Livingstone's (2012) examination of the practices of lesson planning. She concludes that lesson plans have not changed radically enough since ICTs were introduced in classrooms. She argues that this is due to two overriding factors: there is still some way to go to establish convincing evidence for teachers that ICTs improve learning outcomes, and there is confusion over whether they have been installed to support the delivery of traditional education or to instigate a whole new pedagogy.

Whether it is about lesson planning or assignment writing, what is required in new digital learning environments is a framework which focuses on the practices of important educational events. There is a need to focus on the re-organisation of relationships between actors in the new digital learning environments, where the traditional order of the classroom may have been disrupted or transformed into another set of practices altogether.

Carolyn Marvin (1988) in her work *When Old Technologies Were New* argues that there is a kind of re-organisation of relationships brought about by the instalment and utilisation of new technologies. These then reshape power structures and bring new tensions to the fore; these tensions are at their most pronounced when old ways of doing things are carried out alongside newer ways. Writing primarily about electrical communication (early telephone, phonograph, etc.), she states this relationship as follows:

> Electrical and other media precipitated new kinds of social encounters long before their incarnation in fixed institutional form. In their institutionally inchoate manifestations, they inspired energetic efforts to keep outsiders out and insiders under the control of the proper people . . . Classes, families, and professional communities struggled to come to terms with novel acoustic and visual devices that made possible communication in real time without real presence, so that some people were suddenly too close and others much too far away. New kinds of encounters collided with old ways of determining trust and reliability, and with old notions about the world and one's place in it: about the relation of men and women, rich and poor, black and white, European and non-European, experts and publics.
>
> (Marvin, 1988: 5–6)

More recent formulations of 'disruptive pedagogy' (Hedberg, 2011) have applied such ideas to look specifically at the impacts of technologies on education (Christensen *et al.*, 2011). 'Disruption' in this case relates to how new technologies reshape institutional structures and traditional learning and teaching procedures. Disruptive pedagogies can therefore represent a way to understand how traditional and hitherto dominant methods and tools can become dislodged by the incorporation of new technologies and innovative educational practices which stem from them. It is often hoped by proponents of digital media in education that incorporation of technologies in this way can radically transform education and alleviate educational disadvantage through such disruptive practices and innovations.

However, Hedberg (2006) argues that much e-learning practice remains "characterized by transfer and driven by the teacher" (p. 8). He furthermore suggests pedagogies which allow learners to "transcend" conventional tools and institutional strategies towards ICT use to transform the role of the learner "from a passive participant to an active engaged constructor of their own experience" (Hedberg, 2006). Disruptive pedagogies are about aligning pedagogic practices with the potentials offered by digital media tools. This framing, however, does not problematise how disruption actually occurs and how practices with digital media are not always predictable, let alone aligned with technological affordances. These recent formulations using the term 'disruption' are a departure from Clayton Christensen's use and coinage of the term which was in relation to markets and innovations. In Chapter 8, I will revisit the notion of disruption in more detail.

Moving on from the fields of educational technology and disruptive pedagogy, what is needed is a focus on the constantly emerging practices—including literacy practices—of learners who use digital media in real learning scenarios. This is because the digital literacy practices of assignment writing may not necessarily exist in a coherent way, despite their ostensible connection; some may be capricious, others stealthily done. Some may be rehearsed behaviours, or surreptitious workarounds, and occasional circumventions of institutional policies as a learner assumes the role of "an engaged constructor". Nor should we assume that students' digital literacy practices are predictable and readily referable to a framework merely because a group of them are working on a standardised task. The issue is how these digital literacy practices are enacted and how they interact with each other as part of writing strategies and task completion.

Notes

1 A breakdown of the levels of the UK's Qualifications and Credit Framework (QCF) for the participants' of this study can be found at http://www.accredited qualifications.org.uk/qualifications-and-credit-framework-qcf.html.

2 There is, to date, no clear and agreed upon definition of what 'educational technology' means. A related term, 'technology-enhanced learning', is also plagued by a multitude of unshared understandings of its use. According to Jones (2015), they can be generalised as superordinate terms to describe inquiry within computer science, psychology, and social sciences (see Jones, 2015: 9–11). A further critique of the underlying assumptions of these terms is provided by Bayne (2015).

Part II

3 Sara's Assignment on Childcare

Background

Abbeydale College is a large college located in a densely populated and multicultural area in the north of England. According to a quality inspection report published immediately before this research was carried out, the college has just over 19,000 enrolled students, of whom around 3,000 are 16- to18-year-olds. Over half of this particular age group are enrolled as full-time students, with 31% describing themselves as belonging to a minority ethnic group and 61% from socially deprived areas of the region. Diversity remains a distinctive feature of this college's provision and identity, and it explicitly remains committed to widening student participation and recruiting from under-represented groups within its constituency.

About two-thirds of the college's teaching provision is directed to its vocational courses; the remainder are part of its growing higher education, or university, provision for which it continually tries to recruit nationally. It now also receives a proportionately higher level of national funding compared to other colleges for this branch of its activities. In terms of the institution-wide ICT facilities, the college received overall positive quality inspection reviews on how its VLE platform is adopted and used to engage students, but most of this positive feedback is related to the staff's use of the VLE for disseminating resources and announcing course-related issues. Little mention is made of the students' use of the VLE. This feedback was particularly positive for courses in the department of health and social care, which is where I observed Sara's classes and then her assignment work.

The Course

The course that Sara studies is the CACHE (Council for Awards in Care, Health and Education) Level 3[1] certificate in caring for children. The course has a distinct vocational dimension, a learner age group of around 18–22 years, and is assessed through a series of externally set writing assignments. Most of these assignments are completed in classroom-based workshops in which the teacher and learners negotiate writing content. The teacher of the course designs the assignment tasks, which are based on an externally set framework by CACHE. The course is designed to prepare the students with the requisite knowledge and skills to work with children and young people, and many go on to work in what in the UK is referred to as the 'Early Years and Foundation Stage' (EYFS) sector.

The course consists of practical and taught sessions, assessment by regular assignments that meet specific CACHE criteria (such as the one recorded and explored for this case study), observations of learners undertaking work-like tasks, and work placements. Students are also expected to participate in enrichment activities which form part of the course's broader activities. These include such things as 'drug awareness' and fundraising for children's charities. These are seen as external to the course but essential elements of childcare as a vocational field and part of the broader preparations for being a childcare professional.

The following vignette was reconstructed from a detailed set of field notes, as I was getting to know the college, the course, and the culture of digital media use at a general institutional level.

Upon entering the classroom for the first time, I am taken by the wall displays which are colour-rich and about topics related to the course: childcare ethics, disability, contraception, to name a few. One particular display (shown in Figure 3.1) makes an explicit connection to communication as a fundemental component of the course and, as branches on a tree, names all the forms of communication that students practice. There is also a display of the 'class guidelines' and piles of textbooks at the far back of the class.

There is one fascinating technological exception to this print-rich environment: a display of 'virtual babies'. These are dolls which are offered to Level 2 students of this course in order for them to take home and, through their use, learn the basics of childcare. These dolls are called 'virtual babies' and are sophisticated doll machines (see Figure 3.2) that have functions to behave like human babies and which the Level 2 students must take home and 'look after'. This is to test their abilities to change nappies and tend to crying, etc., and also for them to have a taste of the kinds of activities this line of work could entail.

Later on I ask staff about ICT-related documentation (policies, etc.), and the teacher hands two documents over to me which she says I will be interested in. She hasn't read them properly herself, but she is convinced that they are what I am looking for. These are the colleges' 'ICT acceptable use policy' and the 'staff digital communications policy'. I am interested in knowing the extent to which they are adopted and adhered to by staff and, more importantly, the students. One of the documents clearly states that it is for staff use in relation to their web-based interactions with students, yet the teacher mentions that she has not even read the document, or has merely skimmed over it at best. This is despite it being issued to her nearly a year ago. Relatedly, she mentions that one tutor was suspended recently for disparaging the college in a Facebook status update. Such actions are clearly stated in the policy as warranting disciplinary proceedings.

Figure 3.1 Classroom Display on Student Commutation Practices

Both the students and the teachers of the college are encouraged to use ICTs for course-related activities, but their use is strictly dictated by two documents: a *staff digital communications policy* and an ICT *acceptable use policy*, which together spell out the purpose, scope, and guidance for using digital media whilst on the college premises and for college purposes. The documents provide what the college describes as 'safety guidance' on the 'phenomenal explosion' of social media in everyday use, how to best

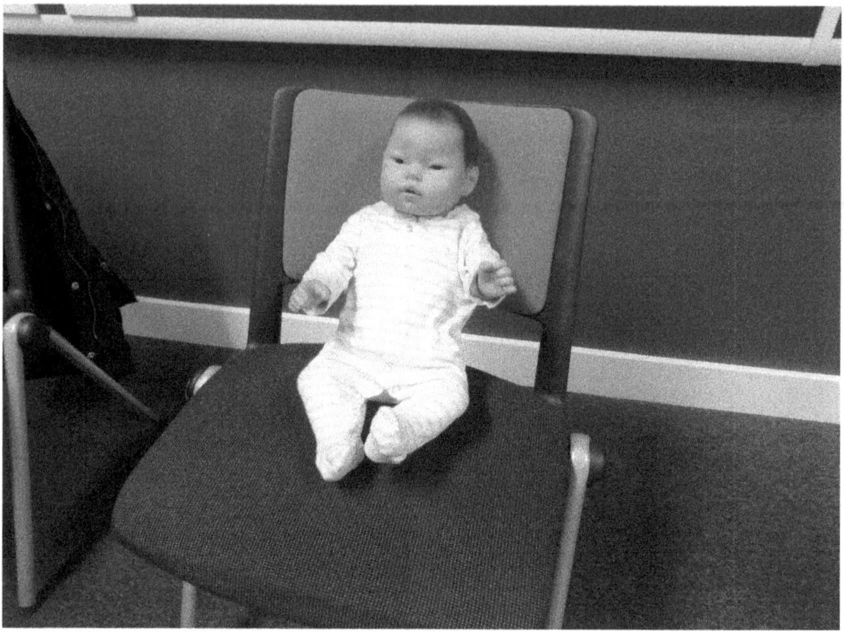

Figure 3.2 Virtual Baby on Display in Sara's Classroom

appropriate digital media for learning and teaching, and protocols for their use. Later in this account, I consider the salience of these policy documents as agentive forces which shape the kinds of digital literacy practices during Sara's assignment writing.

Through initial observations of the class, I noticed that the sessions are divided into two parts. Part one is a largely teacher-led and lecture-like session where the teacher outlines and elaborates on assessment criteria and their application in the work of a childcare practitioner. This is followed by a second session immediately after an interval break where the students have a lot more freedom to get on with written assignment work and projects using laptops. This is borne out in the vignette that follows, which is drawn from my field notes on a session:

An initial, largely teacher-led, lesson lasts for around 60 minutes. This is followed by a two-hour writing workshop in which the learners work largely autonomously on their ongoing assignments which must meet the criteria of the unit as set out in their handouts and displayed on the whiteboard. The session I am observing focusses specifically on child protection policies, and is connected to a future assignment.

This writing session (2:45p.m.–4:45p.m.) follows immediately after an interval break. Here the students have a lot more freedom to get on with their assignment work and most of them do make use of this time. It is independent assignment work facilitated with laptops, and the teacher moves around the room monitoring and helping individually. A special trolley (known and referred to by staff and students as "the trolley") which collectively holds, charges, and stores the departmental laptops is wheeled in by a technician. A unique feature of this session is that as soon as the trolley is pushed in and set up, the whole atmosphere in the room changes, and such things as personal devices (phones, mp3 players, etc.) and the listening of music have now all of a sudden become permitted. Headphones seem to be plugged in, and music is being listened to.

All the students get up and collect their laptops from the trolley, set up at their desks, and begin the staccato 'pitter patter' upon logging on, etc. This second part of the lesson brings a change in tempo, noise, and talk, with the teacher monitoring and discussing more individually as she spends the entire time moving around the room. Some students are not talking at all, just typing and getting on with it. More talk around the topic and more talk on any topic, including on boyfriends, is going on. It seems the switch from the first component of the lesson has brought an entire shift in the mood, manner, and method of the class in the second session.

In the vignette, a definite and marked change of pace occurs in the writing session which follows the more lecture-like session before it. The deployment of the laptops (which are wheeled in on 'the trolley', see Figure 3.3) in the second, writing-focussed session brings with it the sudden permitted use of their smaller 'cousins' in the world of materialities: smartphones, mp3 players, iPods, etc. Listening to music and completing other practices

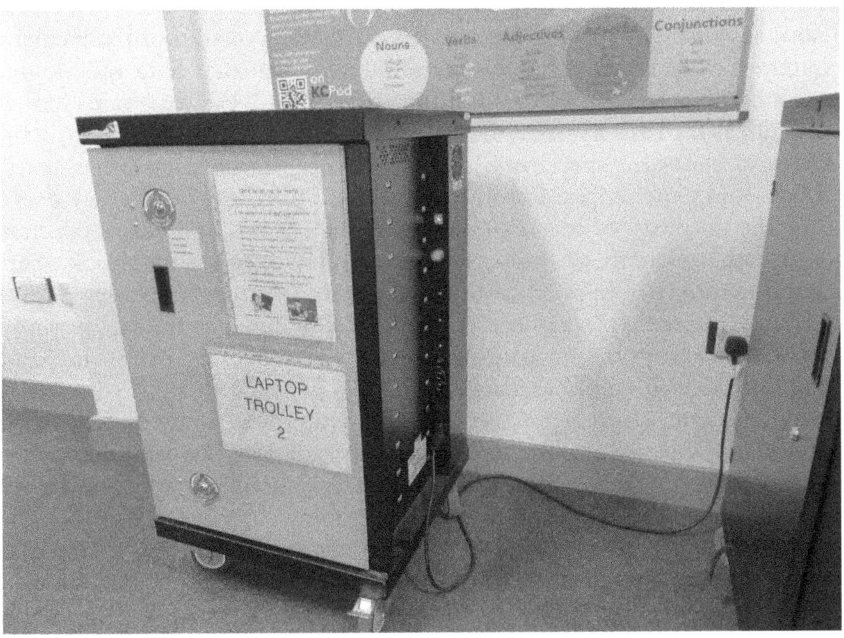

Figure 3.3 The Laptop Trolley with Machines Charged and Ready to Use

through the devices raises the question of which practices are precisely 'off task' and 'on task' for Sara. This is something I will come to later as part of a discussion on *performativity*.

It is important to note that personal devices, especially when they are used in this way, are ordinarily forbidden by the acceptable use policy and norms of the college. This was diligently abided by in the lecture-like session earlier. However, a host of actors have now entered the scene, and the sociomaterial work of the assignment as its writing begins to unfold is radically different in manner to the kind of work which occurred before the interim break. The wheeling in of the laptop trolley becomes a symbolic shift in mode, method, and culture. It is an actant which acts as a hub to connect the classroom and the work carried out within it to a multitude of other actors that are now able to *irrupt* into the scene (see Chapter 8 for more on irruption).

Sara is about to embark on her assignment, and her digital literacy practices include work carried out across a range of platforms, devices, and time frames. For various reasons, her practices extend the sociomaterial assemblage into multiple places. I will discuss specific aspects of these practices in the coming sections.

Sara's Assignment

In this account, the assignment writing begins via a series of bullet points displayed on the whiteboard. These points are a simplified version of the assessment criteria that the teacher gave out to the students, discussed in the previous session. The display features an elaborated version of the particular criterion to be covered for the current assignment that Sara was doing, criterion E6 (see the vignette that follows and Figure 3.4). The origins of this text stretch as far back as when the criteria were written, most likely by item writers and childcare specialists, and was likely drawn from other texts, locations, and experiences. But in the 'here and now' of this literacy event and for the purposes of this assignment writing, Sara's immediate practice is to copy the contents of the text of the display into her notebook. This is a continuation of her practice of taking notes from the previous session and asking questions throughout it. In the following account, we see how she then draws from these various elements, and others, to commence and accomplish the writing of her assignment.

In the vignette, Sara begins writing the assignment immediately upon being seated. With an almost perfunctory automation, she sits, draws her USB flash drive out of her pocket, plugs it in, and opens up previous work.

The session begins when all the students enter the classroom, having just had their break. The teacher announces, "Ladies, bags off the tables". They are quite chatty at this point and setting themselves up for the writing session.

Unit 18: Working With Babies From Birth to 12 Months		
Criteria	*Grading Criteria*	*Guidance*
E5	Describe the role of the practitioner in meeting the particular needs of babies in the chosen type of setting (group care *or* home-based care).	Give information about the responsibilities of the practitioner in *either* group care *or* home-based care. Responsibilities should relate to the chosen care setting and could include establishing relationships with baby and parents, identifying and planning to meet baby's holistic needs, observation and recording of development, supervision, resources/ equipment, routines, other children . . .
E6	Show how the child protection policies and procedures in the setting protect and safeguard the babies.	Information about how child protection policies and procedures of the setting protect babies. This may include observation/recording/ reporting, recognising signs of abuse, confidentiality, rights of child, welfare of child, work with parents, teamwork . . .
E7	Explain the importance of well-planned care routines and the key worker System.	Give reasons why well-planned care routines and the key worker system benefit babies in early year's settings. This may include links with home, individual needs identified/met, security and consistency, babies learn to predict what is to happen, overall development and learning, relationships with parents, shared information, confidence and trust . . .

Figure 3.4 The Unit Criteria for Childcare Assignments

The current unit on the syllabus they are covering in this class is unit 18, and the criterion to be covered is E6 (Child Protection Policies). This is up on the board as well as in front of Sara at her desk. But instead of carefully reading the text of the unit, without a moment's hesitation, Sara opens an assignment from a previous unit criterion (E5). She plugs in her USB drive and locates and opens files and folders organised as follows: CACHE Childcare and Education > Childcare 2nd Year > Unit 18 > E5 > filename: 'working with babies from birth to 12 months'. These are well organised files and folders mobilised immediately into action on her screen.

She scrolls through sections of the texts of previous assignments, highlights and deletes sections, and incorporates other sections into a new file within the same folder of collected work (saved as 'E6'), while keeping elements of each text. What follows is a swift movement between files that are open in different windows on her laptop. Judiciously archived previous work allows her to open her files quickly, move between them, and interweave the contents of a previous assignment into the current file. She does this whilst discussing henna styles with Lauren (the student beside her). The writing of the new assignment is now well under way.

Without a moment's hesitation, Sara opens the assignment from a previous unit criterion (E5) as a basis upon which to begin her work. The validation of previous writing as a basis for 'what works' is a decision she has made quite instantaneously based on her regular assignment-writing routine,[2] and it is a judgement of strategy based on the similarity between the criterion being covered (E6) and the assignment before it (criterion E5). What becomes written by Sara is her own synthesis and *recontextualisation* of this previous assignment. It therefore becomes an important part of this assemblage, as shall be discussed later. Its font, layout, etc., are all a validation upon which to begin the new assignment.

While previous work plays an important role in Sara's overall writing strategy and in how the assignment takes its shape, further scrutiny reveals a general ad hoc use of material artefacts available at hand as well interactions with a multitude of actors who are not always in situ. It is an assemblage of practices extended into multiple spatial and temporal realms constituting actors such as those listed next. The list is broadly in order of how they emerged with some overlap:

- The directives of a college policy,[3] distributed to all staff and students upon induction, which spells out and limits the purpose and scope for using digital media at the college. In this policy, 'social' and 'non-educational chat' are considered 'unacceptable' activities.
- The utilisation of previous assignments as a template and validation upon which to begin the current task and reformulating text extracts from them.
- Interactions with Google searches and its algorithm's suggestions.
- Discussions with the teacher and Lauren (beside her) to confirm or clarify task requirements, instructions, and search results.
- Interactions with government online resources, reports, etc.
- Social networking ties and chats with friends online. These communication practices become capricious violations of the college policy, but nonetheless assignment related.
- Interactions with school websites and drawing from their texts, such as a prospectus and inspection report from the website of the school in which she carried out her work placement.

These actors contribute to the assignment's completion and point to the various practices that were part of Sara's endeavour to seek out content, apply a certain amount of discernment, synthesise it, and represent it for her writing. All of these things and more, as elaborated in the vignettes that follow, were part of Sara's endeavour to garner information for her writing in order to get it done. These aspects are outlined and discussed further in the coming sections as Sara 'assembles' her assignment.

Assembling the Assignment

We see the event beginning as a set of instructions for an assignment which is issued by the teacher and elaborated on extensively in the previous session. The whiteboard display has remained up, as the students have had their interim break before the writing session. This guidance is then transmitted by means of the teacher's verbal instructions, her notes on the whiteboard in the lecture preceding the writing session, and the outline of the unit criterion relating to this assignment. The criterion being written about is E6: *Show how the child protection policy and procedures in the setting protect and safeguard the babies* (see Figure 3.4). According to the unit description, the assignment must show how child protection policies and procedures of the workplace setting protect babies. This would include evidence obtained through observations, reporting, recognising signs of abuse, and understanding protective rights of children.

In the vignette that follows, Sara is asking lots of questions about the assignment. These questions are directed to her immediate classmates primarily and then to the teacher. The questions concern the content of the assignment (the Children's Act 1989) and how they relate to the criteria, but her motives for asking are to ascertain the extent to which this content relates to the content of previous work. This is an important part of her strategy for tackling this assignment task, as is indicated in the previous vignette as well as the one that follows:

Sara starts discussing the assignment's contents, repeating the same question she asked the teacher to Lauren beside her. She glances at the whiteboard instructions, her notes from the previous session, and her screen continuously. This includes guessing and working out what is required in terms of format and submission. She discusses the contents of the legislation (the Children's Act 1989) with Lauren. Lauren says that she will 'just copy and paste . . . ' from a similar previous assignment, ' . . . cos it's our own words anyway'. The teacher hears this and walks over to ask if anyone at the table needs any help.

Sara now opens up another previous assignment, one which related to unit 4 (we are now at unit 18), as this contains previous work on the Children's Act 1989. They are instructed by the teacher to 'not just copy and paste' and told that this criterion only carries five marks and that they just need to mention the main legislation acts (e.g. the Children's Act). This is because Sara and Lauren are not sure how many and which policies/acts they are supposed to write about. The teacher clarifies that it is the 'settings' which dictate this—i.e. where they have worked before or done their work placement.

Nevertheless, there is some sort of an understanding between Sara and Lauren that they have discovered a 'shortcut' method of getting the assignment done. This leads to a swift movement between files already open in different windows on her laptop; judiciously stored previous work through Sara's meticulous and personal digital archiving allows her to open her files, move between them, and interweave the contents of a previous assignment into the current file. She does this whilst discussing 'henna' styles with Lauren.

She stops typing, pauses, and then refers to Google for information on 'child protection'. The algorithm's interruptions and suggestions leave her confused, so she asks Lauren and the teacher again for help.

Previous work serves an important role for Sara throughout writing this assignment, and we can draw upon John Law's (2012) notion of 'collateral realities' to better understand this. Collateral realties are, according to Law, those realities that get done along the way—that is, serendipitously, unintentionally, or incidentally. When she considers how to approach the assignment and to understand what is expected of her, Sara thinks back and refers to the regulations and patterns that have informed her previous work—her previous assignments. These provide Sara with validation of how to work in the present: outlining the font to be used, stylistic considerations (headings, title, etc.), and the appropriate style and the length of the piece. Sara draws on practices from a previous time, a different place, and undertaken with a different intention—and their collateral realities; these realities also extend beyond the immediate temporal domain of her present and into the past as she mobilises previous work into purposeful (re)use here. Importantly, there is a tension between her actual practices of assignment writing, and the perceived acceptable practice of college classroom culture. This is where the notion of collateral realities becomes most interesting, and we will return to it in more detail later.

How the topics of previous assignments relate to the current task is something which emerges throughout the writing of this assignment, as Sara relies on her documents of previous work carefully organised and archived on her pen drive. This inter-relationality of topics is characteristically represented in a departmental corridor display which depicts how issues such as government policies, disability, prejudice, and language development are recurring themes within the vocational field of childcare, and some of which have emerged in different assignment tasks to varying degrees. These topics are displayed to remind learners of how they interface with the work of childcare. Previously written content related to these recurring themes is often retained in past assignments, to be meticulously kept by Sara and mobilised into action in situations like this one. The life of one assignment, therefore, segues into another. This is, as she testifies in our later interview discussion, a type of rehearsed behaviour and part of her writing tactic (see interview extract that follows). What matters is that she is drawing on realities beyond the immediate site with her own experience of prior practices for validation. We were watching such a moment in the recording as we spoke:

Ibrar: Did you get stuff from a previous assignment?
Sara: First, when I started writing I was just blank coz the way she was explaining, like, you need to include different settings and that. But later on when I looked into it and then when I looked back on the work then I clicked on that and knew what to do coz I'd done it previously.
Ibrar: So you knew something about this topic but you needed to get some background?
Sara: Yeah . . .
Ibrar: How else did you get that background? From Google?
Sara: Yeah.
Ibrar: Did you have an outline in your head of how you're going to do it? . . . Or did it just slightly develop?
Sara: Just slightly developed as I went on.

As Law (2012) notes, both the act of note-taking, giving a talk, and writing down a version of that talk create and describe different "putative realities": the reality of the assignment as understood and created by the teacher's verbal instructions, the version on the whiteboard, and what exists and evolves on Sara's screen. Each retransmission of the idea, by what it includes and excludes about the task, and how the task relates to the end purpose of the aim of meeting criterion E6 for the assignment, are enacting multiple versions of what, if we approached the matter from a *representationalist* perspective, appear to be the same (or a singular) thing—i.e. a singular assignment. It is unsurprising that Sara feels the need to ask the same clarification questions continually. Previous work is based on a network of practices that forms a convenient safety net to fall back on, at least for now.

Fifteen minutes into the session, Sara is still considering how to integrate the contents of previous assignments into the current one. She opens a group of files and, as a tactic, scrolls through them while discussing with Lauren what particular aspects of the previous files (on 'legislation' and 'policies and practices') relate to the work that needs to be done, which aspects do not, and the amount of marks allocated. The requirements of the current assignment, at this stage, are being negotiated with the criterion, previous criteria, a previous assignment, Sara and Lauren's prior knowledge, and guesswork between all of these elements.

Immediately prior to this, Sara was busy figuring out what is required of her and asking the teacher and her immediate peer (Lauren). There is an obvious task here to be completed: an assignment. But there remain a multitude of other subsidiary tasks contained within it: to search the web for certain government policies, to synthesise the way these policies have been implemented in the 'setting' (where Sara did her placement), etc. Some of this is guesswork, and guesswork of varying sorts is a continuing theme during this process. Sara's guessing about what the teacher's instructions entail for her, guessing what the teacher interprets from the criteria, and guessing how her setting would implement the legislation. Perhaps the teacher is also guessing in how the assessment criteria should be addressed in her understanding of the assignment and how it is to be written (based on her previous experience). Perhaps the writers of the criteria also made guesses about the kinds of things to include for this specialist vocational area in their design of the rubrics.

Nevertheless, for Sara, to 'copy and paste' (i.e. from previous assignments) then becomes a viable strategy suggested by Lauren who is sitting next to her. The tactics emerging, therefore, are both explicitly stated (such as the teacher's instruction to web search, among other things), and also implicit and muttered under the breath of Lauren ("just copy and paste . . . cos it's our own words anyway").

Garnering Information

Sara needed to garner information for her writing. We have already looked at a few sources she makes use of in order to achieve this, such as her teacher, her notes, and her classmate. In the vignette that follows, around 20 minutes into the assignment, Sara invokes another actant for assistance:

Sara refers to Google to search for details about some legislation which she needs to include in her assignment. As she types 'child protection . . .' the algorithm's auto-complete stops her mid-word to suggest the following:

child protection act
child protection policy
child protection plan
child protection training
child protection register
child protection procedures

Although this is not the first time the algorithm has spoken back to her, on this occasion, she pauses at the auto-complete suggestions and stumbles, confused about what it is that she should be looking for. She turns to Lauren to say, 'There it is, look, child protection act'. The teacher intervenes to clarify that 'child protection' is the name of the policy, which is contained within the 'Children's Act', and that there is no such 'children's act', at least within the UK.

Sara's confusion lies in a 'child protection act 1999' which she has seen and been reading about online, courtesy of the direct help of Google's suggestions. Unbeknownst to her yet, this piece of legislation is from Australia. This is clarified eventually as the teacher comes over to provide an explanation.

The teacher tells them about how, for the assignment, they need to explicate the policies as understood and implemented by their settings—i.e. where they worked (or did their work experience)—and that they should use work-based documentation as the source. The policies for Sara's setting are stored on the school's website. But she also decides to contact a friend on her phone (via Facebook) to check on this.

During this point in the assignment writing, Sara used the Google search engine to search for information to include in her work. As she types into the search box, the search engine suggests results based on Google's powerful and complex algorithm and its *PageRank* system (Brin & Page, 2012). For our purposes, this algorithm is an actant and actor network in its own right—one that is organised by software engineers at the Google offices in San Jose (California, USA) and therefore far removed from Sara's classroom. Yet here it has been mobilised into the classroom space and brought with it a whole new set of implications—and digital literacy practices—in this emerging sociomaterial assemblage. The Google algorithm is an important part of any writer's searching practices and is a continuously developing[4] artificial intelligence programme which works by relying on over 200 unique signals or 'clues' that make it possible to guess what someone is searching for. These signals include things such as the newness of content, the searcher's region, and device being used. An additional component of the search engine is the assigning of a numerical weighting to linked sets of documents in the web through PageRank.

This linking system gives more credence in its search results to sites that are often linked to by influential sites. This is part of the calculus which drives PageRank and subsequently drives to reach the top of the search results for websites and marketing companies (Steiner, 2012). Taken together, this actant's intrusion here has implications on many levels for Sara's work. Sara's choices as she navigates the interface of the search results (Figure 3.5) are doubtless influenced by the calculus of PageRank and the agencies, financial and otherwise, which position one link above another in the list.

Sara spends a great deal of time hunting for information in this way online, and in every case, there are links thrown up at her in the search results. This is the intervention of the algorithm working out what it 'thinks' she wants or should be viewing. She tends to click the first link offered, but not always, as she browses through web pages belonging to the UK government's 'Department for Education'. She then tries with the search terms "child protection . . ." until she is interrupted again by the algorithm. This interruption is shown in Figure 3.5, in which we see Sara, Lauren, the teacher, and Google all differing over the issue of "child protection . . ." for the purposes of this assignment.

Sara's confusion in the previous vignette lay in her search for a 'child protection act 1999', which she has been directed to via Google, only to be told

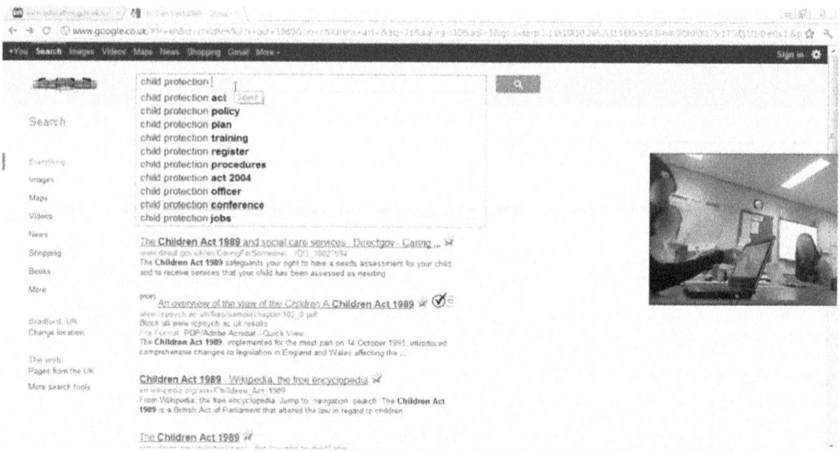

Figure 3.5 Sara, Lauren, the Teacher, and Google Differ on 'Child Protection'

that Google's suggestion is incorrect. This was because she was lead to legislation from a country other than the UK that was subsequently not relevant to her assignment. The teacher then tells the students that, for the assignment, they need to explicate the policies as understood and implemented by their *settings*—i.e. where they have worked (or undertook their work-experience internship). Moreover, they should use the work-based documentation of the setting as the source to give their assignment some individual context. The policies for Sara's setting are stored on the website of the school in which she carried out her internship. She is then directed by the teacher to access those websites, but Sara has another option in mind at the end of the vignette—another one of her shortcut strategies to get the work done (see the section titled 'Unacceptable Use' in this chapter). But for now, the algorithm's interruptions deserve some more scrutiny in this part of the account.

The algorithm's interruptions and suggestions left her confused and far away from her original task, such that the teacher was forced to intervene and get her on task again. Thus the programming behind an algorithm is a crucial part of the assemblage as it interacts with other actors: the teacher's instructions (both oral and written), the friend's advice, the acceptable use policy, the previous assignments, etc. Sara receives a clarification as to what she needs to look for and has a better idea about what she needs to do, but no less than 30 minutes into the task duration.

Another way of looking at the algorithm's interruptions is as integral parts of an interaction. In the digital multimodal transcript excerpt in Figure 3.6, presented using a software called ELAN,[5] we can see a clip of data showing Sara's interactions with Google whilst web searching in a slightly different way to how it has been described already. Upon repeated

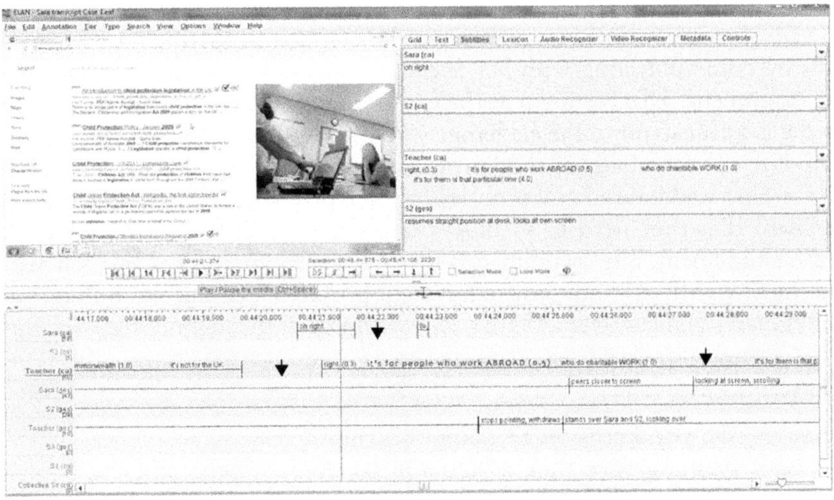

Figure 3.6 ELAN Multimodal Transcript Screenshot Showing Pauses Whilst Interacting With Web Pages

viewing of the data clip, slowed down and expanded by the transcription of gesture and bodily movement, we observe that pauses occur between turns during web searching and the ensuing discussion about class work, depicted by the ♦ symbol.

The pauses correspond with Sara's exchanges with web-based, actors (websites, algorithms, etc.) during writing and suggest that an algorithm's suggestions and interruptions instantiate a turn in interaction. The question of whether lexicality is a necessary feature of a turn is important here, and the notion of the 'material' as interlocutor or interactant is something which has been discussed to some extent in ethnomethodological research within the field of human-computer interaction (e.g. Dourish & Button, 1998) and technologically inflected ANT studies (e.g. Nicholls, 2009). This research is led by the Latourian injunction to follow actors and to pursue "new unexpected actors that have more recently popped up and which are not yet bona fide members of 'society' " (Latour, 2005: 22). In this vein, in the transcript screenshot, Sara's interacting with Google's algorithm would appear as moments of silence in a conventional transcript. Yet here they appear as key moments of interaction in the representational system adopted; the materiality, in a sense, has a 'voice', in addition to the other interactions and 'voices' around this assemblage, some of which are not represented in a traditional linguistic transcription.

The next section addresses the action Sara takes at the end of the last vignette. It explores the implications of her contacting a friend via Facebook to ask about an issue regarding her work settings for her assignment.

Unacceptable Use

As Sara gets well into her assignment, she engages in specific social conventions by communicating with her friend, whilst inquiring about an aspect of the assignment. This is shown at the end of the previous vignette, and the following is a transcript of the exchange which shows how this occurred. After a period of web searching on child protection legislation, the teacher has walked over to Sara and Lauren and is outlining the requirements of the task, reminding them that they need to include a discussion of child protection policies in the assignment. She recommends the policies as interpreted by their work placement ('settings'), but Sara is having a problem locating this online. Lauren regularly glances over at Sara's screen and back throughout the exchange.

Transcript Extract 1

Sara: Do you know we're doing this right?
Teacher: Making sure they're actually covered by what they're actually saying.
Sara: You know where it says you have to include the policies? Do we have to look at our setting's policies?
Teacher: Yeah, yeah, yeah, or any policies that you're familiar with have you collected anything in err (.) for your pr [personal reflective] diaries on policies?
Teacher: Do you remember what you've got?
Sara: I think I still got them at home. I'll have to check them.
Teacher: Anything to do with child protection?
Sara: Cos you know the place where I'm at now they said that the policies and procedures are on the Internet cos they said we don't have them cos when I asked for them paper based they said it's on Internet.
Lauren: Can you ask anyone?
Sara: Yeah I'm going to ask my friend, on Facebook, Amarah; she's there, heh heh.
(Sara then proceeds to contact her friend through her phone held under her desk to inquire about the policies)
[end of clip]

By using the digital artefact of her smartphone to communicate with her peers who are in other locations, Sara turns a digital artefact of her own possession into an actor, which, through the software and hardware governing the media being used, renders these interactions distinct in particular ways from the other interactions in the classroom which are through the college's sanctioned institutional technologies. Her smartphone (and its software and hardware) are now mobilised for use in this assemblage. Every part of this scenario of using the Facebook platform and her phone presents a tension between an institutionally validated understanding of digital media use, as outlined in the college's 'acceptable use policy' (see Figure 3.7), and Sara's casual flouting and circumventing of it.

Her assignment is thereby further modified and influenced, but this time by another dimension to her digital literacy practices through describing her task to her friend, who has then given information back. Each of these elements feed into the digital literacy event, illustrating the way in which digital media in a classroom can serve as a conduit for cross-network (e.g. personal and curricular) literacy practices. It begs to asked, therefore, what is exclusively *vernacular*, *social*, or *academic* in the digital literacy practices of Sara's assignment?

Notably, personal use of social networking during class time is not approved by the college and is stated quite clearly in documentations such as the 'acceptable use policy' as prohibited for students using ICTs in the college premises and during classes. The college's policy spells out the purpose, scope, and guidance for students using digital media whilst situated on the college premises and carrying out curricular work. It predominantly provides safety guidance concerning the phenomenal explosion of social media such as Facebook in everyday use and how to best appropriate its use for learning.

Unacceptable Content

You must not seek, view, download, publish, transmit or communicate content that is:
Threatening, offensive, abusive, libellous, harassing, pornographic, sexist, racist.

And/or which relates to:
Terrorism, cults, dating, drugs, gambling, criminal skills (including software hacking), social chat, jokes or chain mail that is not related to your course social groups, personal business (such as any private work that you do).

Unacceptable Activities

You must not:
Attempt to hack the College or other systems; simulate other users (pretend to be them, or use their login); use anonymous access (where you cannot be identified); tamper with workstation addresses, settings or software; use College IT facilities purely for private, social or personal business use within timetabled study time; download or use games over the network, other than software installed and approved for learning purposes

Personal Use

Personal Use of IT Facilities:
The College is prepared to accept limited personal use of the IT Facilities, **outside** time-tabled class time. This might include research, personal finance, family appointments/communication, social networking etc.

Figure 3.7 Extracts From the College's ICT Acceptable Use Policy

Sara most definitely broke some of these rules in her interactions, as the policy states that 'social' and 'non-educational' chats are unacceptable activities alongside, in another part of the same document, "using the ICT facilities for private, social or personal business purposes within work or study time". It further states that students must not use their private/home email addresses to send mail from the college premises, that they must always use the email address allocated by the college, and only use the Internet for 'legitimate activities' associated with work or study at the college.

It seems that the college policy statements make a clear and categorical distinction between legitimate activities with digital media associated with work or study at the college and personal use—one can interfere with the other. As an actant forcing its agenda in this assemblage, one could say that it is trying to tell other actors what to do and how to do it. A harsh example of what can happen when such policies are not adhered to is the case of a college teacher (mentioned earlier in this chapter) who was disciplined for disparaging comments about his employer on Facebook. Sara, on the other hand, has an assignment to get on with, and her educational and professional future depend on this. The teacher, for her part, has her targets to meet and wants this assignment completed before the next unit criterion is looked at for the following session. Both of them are under different pressures to attain the same goal: a passable and fit-for-purpose assignment.

Another thing to note in this account of Sara's assignment is that the policy also mentions using Moodle, the college's institutional VLE, as a 'risk-free alternative' to Facebook for communicating with students. It mentions safety but doesn't state any examples of what a potential danger is. The college does not actively encourage Facebook use, but recognises that some tutors utilise it as an alternative teaching tool to improve communication and engagement with students. This practice is discouraged but not proscribed and is subject to strict measures if misused.

After the writing session was recorded, I asked Sara to elaborate on how she uses the VLE for the course generally. She spells out her responses to the VLE and to the acceptable use policy more generally in the following interview extract:

Ibrar: There's the VLE isn't there? Do you use Moodle at work or at college?
Sara: What's that?
Ibrar: You have Moodle don't you for your class work?
Sara: They told us that website and our login and password. I don't even know it [Laughter]
Ibrar: How come? So how do you discuss things about your course?
Sara: You don't need to know it; people only use what they need to use. Yeah Moodle's where you login and get your work or something. We just use Facebook for all that.
Ibrar: Who?

Sara: All us lot.
Ibrar: How did that start?
Sara: I don't know. We just kept on doing it from the start. They keep telling us to use college email and that Moodle thing, but to be honest, I don't even know my password! [Laughter]

Sara's embracing of social networking in her personal life has allowed its use to infiltrate into her course activities as she uses it for discussions instead of the institutionally validated and preferred Moodle site. When asked about her social networking activities, Sara mentioned them in the contexts of her home, college, and work spheres. It seems that friendships initiated and maintained in personal and/or work spheres, for Sara, encouraged camaraderie in the classroom, extending to professional networking through work placements and also personally. She positions herself in multifaceted ways in the classroom doing the assignment: as a seeker of information, as a student seeking assistance, as a friend asking a favour, etc. The classroom digital literacy event is therefore a multi-layered and unbound phenomenon with ephemeral infiltrations of Sara's digital literacy practices that would be otherwise deemed 'personal' or 'vernacular'.

The interview component of the data collection for this research also included a Venn diagram activity with an icon mapping exercise. This is a participatory technique (Emmel, 2008) and substantiated in prior research of this kind (e.g. Ivanič *et al.*, 2009). This activity allowed me to explore some of the themes that emerged through our discussion about her assignment and her practices of digital literacy more generally. A picture of Sara's Venn diagram is in Figure 3.8, where she arranged the icons as we talked. Sara's placing of her icons of digital media usage across the prototypical contexts of her home, college, and work spheres substantiate some of the practices during her assignment.

For example, Sara described how her 'outside' of college digital habits have infiltrated her classroom practice and that she tries to use social networking platforms for multiple purposes as much as she can. This is usually to save time and effort, and is shown in the Venn diagram as a group of icons (Hotmail, Facebook, WhatsApp, Twitter) clustered together and occupying the small home/college crossover section. The arrows also show how use of these platforms and tools 'flow' into her college activities despite previously being exclusively home-based practices.

Through using digital media in classroom activities, Sara creatively employs any means at her disposal when getting on with college work. Notably, the Moodle VLE platform of the college remains separately positioned in the Venn diagram. It is solely within the college sphere and even has a sad emoticon next to it—Sara had totally forgotten what it is when I asked her about it in the interview extract presented earlier. The blogging platform, Blogger, is positioned squarely within the 'work' sphere of Sara's digital media practices

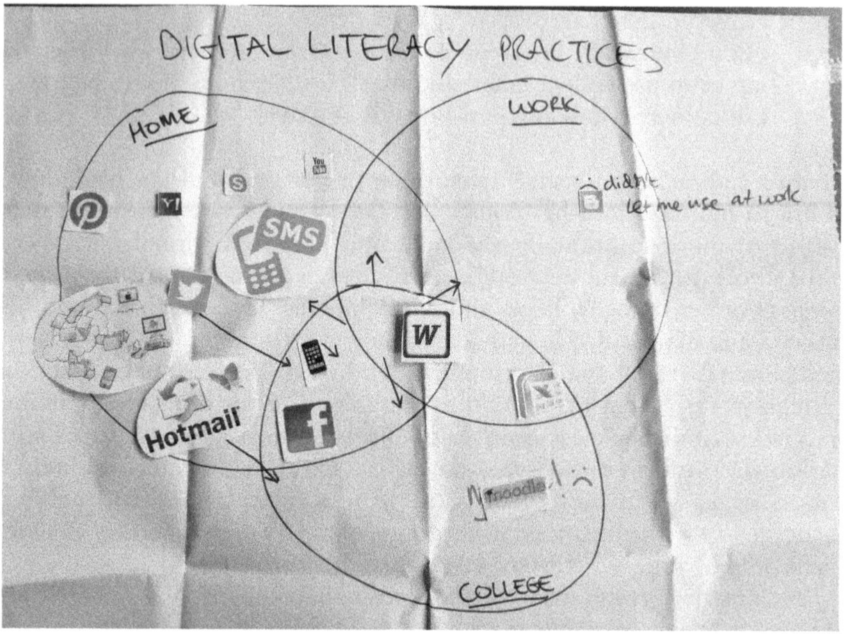

Figure 3.8 Sara's Arrangement of Icons for Digital Media Use Across Home, College, and Work

and has a sad face emoticon beside it. This is because during her work placement as a trainee at a school, she was not allowed to contribute to the school blog despite having a keen interest in doing so. This bothered her, and she wanted to mention it in our discussion. The professional context, like the college, has certain strictures in place about who can do certain activities and, as with the college, these are usually presented as matters of safety and security.

Later in the discussion chapters of the book, I further explore some of these practices of Sara, drawing from findings across the two other case studies of this research as well as proffering new areas of theoretical development.

Looking at Heels

Later in the session, Sara is still searching the Internet for information and guidance on child protection policies. In a previous vignette, we saw how she was directed to the settings of her work placement, and in the vignette that follows, she is still searching for the relevant documentation on the web pages of the school/nursery where she worked:

Forty-five minutes into the assignment, Sara is still searching the web to collate information. She searches for the website of her setting: a local school where she worked on a placement. Somewhere else in the room the teacher asks a student, "What are you googling . . .?" She replies by saying she is "looking at heels", which results in laughter across the room.

Sara scales the menu section of the school website, wondering where she can find information on the child protection policies. She tries the 'Parents and Carers' section first. She then types 'pol;cies and procedures' (with the typo) in the site's search box. No results. Tries again without the typo. No results. Online hunting is becoming difficult.

At the school's website, she now needs to locate where the 'policies and procedures' will be. She clicks on 'About Us', followed by 'quality inspection report' (new window opened), and then 'prospectus'. She then asks Lauren if the policies will be in the prospectus. Lauren replies with "what's a prospectus?"

Scrolling through each of the headings of the prospectus, she struggles to locate anything on child policies and procedures. Whilst scrolling, she is talking about who is dating who, which generates some laughter, with a slightly hysterical moment for Sara. Finally, on one of the pages appears the heading 'child protection' in underlined-bold-italics with a brief paragraph beneath it.

She pauses, leans back in her chair, and continues discussing with Lauren about what amused her earlier, as if giving herself a little break. Did she misunderstand the task earlier? This is a very long time merely figuring out what to do!

Here we see an instance which typifies the kind of freedom accorded to learners when they are left to browse online autonomously, as a student boasts that she is "looking at heels". This boast, which results in laughter across the room, momentarily changes the mood of the whole class. The teacher does not chastise her, although in the next vignette she does chastise another student. She acknowledges these new and web-based actants as now commonplace intruders in classrooms and so does not appear greatly troubled by this brief but disruptive occurrence.

Meanwhile, online hunting is proving quite difficult for Sara. She needs to mention the child protection policies and describe how they have been interpreted by her setting. Locating any mention of them in school quality inspection reports and other documentation is time consuming and, so far, fruitless. A proportionately long time has been spent both figuring out what to do and looking for information online up until this point. But in the next vignette, she finally finds a way through the impasse:

The teacher walks away and chastises another student for wasting time and delaying their work till later and for spending too much time on Facebook.

Meanwhile Sara looks for the policies of the local nursery, but the policy document she needs is at home. She Google searches the name of the nursery and clicks a document for a nursery with a similar name in another city, then saves a pdf report (sixth link down in the results list). Slowly she scrolls through the quality inspection report of the nursery, looking closely for any mention of 'child protection policies'. The teacher continues her chastisement.

One hour into her work, she decides to move documents into relevant folders on the pen drive, organising her documentation.

Having failed to find anything substantially useful for the assignment thus far, Sara goes back to the previous assignments and attempts to garner information which she can copy, paste, and rehash into the current assignment. This is related to the unit criteria of those previous assignments and where the content overlaps. So she begins typing again, reformulating her previous work. Laughter and chatting also ensue around the class

The timing of the lesson is argued over. The teacher insists on the importance of the "extra hour" on the timetable. She then calls out that she will come round to "see what has been done", and walks around the room.

When Sara completes a paragraph, she deletes the paragraph which she reformulated it from (which was also copied and pasted from another assignment). The atmosphere in the classroom in this period is very informal and talkative.

At this point, again, the use of previous assignments is very important when it comes to getting this one done. The moments of mobilisation of previous work are key in the writing of the current assignment. These previous assignments are sociomaterial assemblages which are already hanging together and therefore mobilised by Sara in order to provide a template for the current one. As resources, their validation makes them safe options to invoke and incorporate into this task, especially over free and open web searching, which can lead to nowhere, as she has now realised. The patterns that have informed their completion are reliable prior practices for Sara to fall back on in this moment of impasse.

This process continues for around 20 minutes and is a key stage in this session, as it is the most intense for Sara in terms of actual writing activity. Most of the assignment is written in these 20 minutes: a sudden blast of writing activity after the impasse. This is followed by the end of the session and an instruction to save and store work in a particular way, followed by its submission.

Twenty minutes later, the teacher announces as follows: "Ladies can you finish your sentences and paragraphs and to make sure you save your work and email it to yourself always using your student account. Always email it to yourself using your student account. Just in case".

Sara rushes to get phrases and sentences completed despite errors as many students rise and put their laptops away into the trolley. She then saves her work, again, on her pen drive (not by sending herself an email) and ejects it. And shuts down the laptop. The last 20 minutes of the writing session have been rushed, yet this is where she has completed most of the assignment. She grabs her bag and rushes out the door.

Summary

The methods and strategies behind Sara's assignment-writing tactics rely on networks which break down distinctions between her immediate classroom context and other spaces. By using the Internet to access government reports, she conflates what is inside and outside the a priori reality of 'the classroom'. The writing of the assignment becomes instantiated by a bricolage of practices within events, which in turn connect to other events with their own constituent practices, each and all enacting something else. This aspect of the event, alongside other similar ideas from the other case studies, is further discussed in Chapter 5.

The reports she reads and utilises as background information for her assignment are interpretations of events by their writers who have, in turn, based their own writing on the forms and customs of previous texts. These are texts which are written, read, and interpreted by people in a different spatial and experiential location from Sara reading them in the class. In this way, we can see the potential for Sara's actor network to extend and fit into larger and greater realities beyond the mere period of reading, downloading, copy-pasting, writing, and then uploading. In this respect, the use of previous assignments is also very important to getting this one done. We can view these previous assignments as assemblages which are already 'hanging together', mobilised by Sara in order to instigate and unfold the current one: a writing tactic in itself.

The college does not take account of the richness of Sara's outside-college digital literacy practices, yet the writing workshop provides an easy movement and flow of her literacy practices across domains. It also does not take into account her inside-college use of digital media, as for her to reveal some of this blatantly may render her a rule breaker or even a clever plagiariser. But these practises have a crucial role to play in her getting her work successfully done by the end of the session. These are a kind of 'sub rosa' literacies (Gilmore, 1986) through digital media.

Familiarisation with Sara as a research subject has revealed an impressive commitment to study and achieve in her course assignments, alongside a lack of regard for the imposed way the college wants her to do this. This discussion has demonstrated that Sara engages with multiple sets of practices in assignment writing, based on numerous patterns of relations in her college, work, and home life. This presentation of the account of Sara's assignment writing shows that sometimes one version of a reality, such as an educational 'assignment', can integrate practices of other assemblages. Communications and discussions with friends about music, etc., all form part of the bricolage of digital literacy practices *of* and *for* the assignment; they become fundamentally part of it.

In the dominant culture of the classroom, there is no place for certain digital literacy practices, and there remains a clear hierarchical distinction between 'curricular' usage of digital media and 'social' usage of it. Yet my analysis shows that whilst one reality of the assignment attempts to prevail, it integrates a host of other elements: communications with friends, discussions about music, confusion with a search algorithm, utilisation of previous work, and other digital literacy practices which find their way into, and support the completion of, Sara's assignment. How she then productively negotiates the practices of her assignment writing emerges as a central issue, as it is significant to success in her classroom writing habits. We are drawn into the past as she mobilises previous work for its validation, and into the future as she intends to utilise this very assignment to aid the completion of future work, as such is her practice. We are lead to San Jose (California) as she interacts profusely with a search algorithm to garner information and the wider social and work spheres of her life for the same reasons. There is, therefore, little here which is exclusively 'academic' or 'vernacular' in the way of the literacies for the assignment. These findings are significant as they serve to reinforce the highly complex nature of student engagement with technologies, undermining a monolithic or taxonomic understanding of Sara's 'digital literacy' skills. These themes are further explored in later chapters alongside findings from the other case studies.

Notes

1 For a breakdown of the levels of the UK's Qualifications and Credit Framework see http://www.accreditedqualifications.org.uk/qualifications-and-credit-framework-qcf.html.
2 She confirms this in our follow-up discussion.
3 We can place this first, as it is a document that exists prior to the event and is meant to have a continuing agency on classroom practice with technologies.
4 Google has an R & D budget in excess of $10 billion, most of which goes towards improvements in its search algorithm, artificial-intelligence capabilities, and accessibility of Web content (see http://www.fool.com/investing/general/2015/06/14/5-tech-companies-spending-more-on-rd-than-apple-in.aspx).
5 ELAN is available free from the Language Archive's website: https://tla.mpi.nl/tools/tla-tools/elan/.

4 Anne's Digital Portfolio

Background

Woodale College[1] is a large city campus that has recently merged with two other neighbouring institutions. Another recent and significant development for Woodale College is the appointment of a new principal shortly prior to this research being undertaken and an institution-wide inspection conducted during the same year. These milestones have instigated some interesting new initiatives and projects at the college, such as college-wide ICT improvements, and centre on the strategic aims of the newly merged college establishing itself financially and reformulating its identity as a reputable educational provider in the local area. Both the merger and the new principal's appointment meant that, at the time of carrying out the research, ICT improvements were among the college's top priorities as outlined in its new 'strategic vision' document.

In a recent quality inspection report, more than half of the students in this particular site of the college are described as being from 'disadvantaged postcodes', and the college contains an ethnic mix of students closely mirroring that of the local population. Most course enrolments for this campus (over 5,500 enrolments in the year before this research was carried out) are for vocational courses at the foundation level,[2] followed by the intermediate level, and around a fifth of all enrolments at the advanced level or above. Most enrolments remain in the broad vocational areas of preparation for life and work, retail and commercial enterprise, engineering technology and manufacture, and health and public services. A feature of the site of Woodale College is its growing degree-level provision, run in partnership with two local universities, and its large range of courses for adult vocational education (19+ years).

An inspection report for the college published shortly before the research was conducted stipulated a need to improve ICT facilities across the entire college to cope with the diverse requirements of a greater number of students. This included a call for development opportunities for staff in using digital technologies for teaching. This was deemed even more pertinent since the recent merger, and the various challenges and opportunities which it has brought. The course observed as the second case for this study, described in this chapter, was one that was developed as a direct response to this call for improvement and development of the college's teaching staff. This was borne out in the college's *Information and Learning Technology* (ILT) Standards document, which was an initiative implemented across the entire college to act as a means of monitoring and evaluating the extent to which technology is effectively utilised by teaching staff. The course is the Level 4[3] certificate in *Technology for Learning and Delivery* and was an integral part of this newly merged college's priorities at the time of the research.

The Course

The *Technology for Learning and Delivery* (TFLD) course runs from January to June every year. Course duration is 20 weeks, with sessions every Wednesday evening at 6:00–8:00 p.m. The course was designed for teachers who want to become more proficient and confident in their use of digital media to enhance their teaching practice. Since the recent inspection, the college introduced an institution-wide ILT policy and incorporated it into the strategic vision for its newly merged and cross-regional remit. In the following discussion of Anne's case study, I will draw on how this document may have shaped a particular set of protocols and procedures to be carried out in the performance of the lesson, as well as behaviours and literacy practices supporting the completion of the assignment that Anne needed to complete.

What follows are a series of vignette accounts which draw from the different data sources.[4] These begin with a description of the site, background information on the course and the learners, followed by narrative vignette accounts outlining the writing of Anne's assignment. But first, the vignette extract that follows is based on field notes and was recorded quite early on in the observation phase of the research.

According to the teacher, the prerequisites for the course are that the students must a) demonstrate a minimum level of functional ICT skills as teachers and b) have regular class contact with learners in order to practically demonstrate the technologies they will be discussing and evaluating in the course. All of the course students, therefore, are teachers of various programmes at the college.

On the college website, the qualification is described as "ideal for learning professionals, including learning assistants, looking to qualify as tutors, assessors, lecturers and trainers who are interested in the use of emerging technologies to support teaching and learning". Successful completion of the qualification also allows candidates to progress to professional certification, including schemes such as Certified Membership of the Association of Learning Technologies. The certificate is a vocational qualification, and course assessment is moderated by an external assessor.

The TFLD course was designed as a direct consequence of the dictates of the college's strategic vision document and the ILT service standards, both of which are imposed upon the college with uniformity. These standards are a set of specifications which define and direct effective utilisation of ICT for teaching and learning across the whole college. The course was introduced to help the teaching staff of the college become more acquainted with digital technologies and therefore has direct strategic implications and objectives. How this is played out in the practices of the course itself is indicative of the location of lessons: the highly important 'Flexible Learning Centre' which is one of Woodale College's many investments to facilitating effective ICT usage on campus. College investments at a large scale also have effects on how seriously staff and students apply ICTs in their own college lives. This aspect emerges in the vignette that follows, which is based on field notes of my first lesson observation:

Many of the learners consider themselves novices when it comes to using digital tools for their teaching activities. This becomes apparent during an informal class discussion immediately prior to the lesson. The course is important to them, as they have taken time out to attend it, considering most work full time (and full-time plus). Course members are staff from many different departments across the college. The teacher begins by showcasing a new technology called 'Papershow' supported by notes which are projected onto a whiteboard using an 'e-pen'. Such technological 'show and tell' demonstrations are a recurring theme.

Computers and devices of sorts are pervasive in the 'Flexible Learning Centre', they are your face constantly, like a message is sent out that ICT use is a serious business around here. The equipment seems new, glossy, and shiny, like the course itself. Most of the students on the course pull out the latest iPads and other such writing equipment at their desks, as if in so doing they are stating: 'I have made my investment and I am taking digital technology seriously'.

The purpose of this first lesson is to get the learners to reflect on how they use ICTs in their personal lives and how they can increase and improve on this use for their current teaching practice, and how they can enthuse such an interest in their learners. The underlying theme is that it must be digital technology which enhances the learning and teaching experience. The teacher begins this discussion by talking through an 'e-learning potential' questionnaire to get the learners to reflect on the availability, scope, and utilisation of digital technology in their home and work lives.

Here we see that the participants in the TFLD course are all teaching staff at the college who want—or feel the need—to improve the way they use ICTs in their lessons. Most of them consider themselves novices at using ICT in their personal and professional lives, and this is why they took the course in the first place: so that they can keep up with their learners who appear to be more proficient. These sentiments emerge in the class discussions, as content throughout the course is often related to introductions to new or novel technologies followed by reflective evaluations of their use with students. Naturally, different technologies will have different levels of application in different courses, but such discussions prove reflective and purposeful for the participants of the TFLD course. The conversation itself is a useful exercise for them and prepares them for their forthcoming assignment: the digital portfolio.

The Digital Portfolio

Assessment for the course is carried out through each student's creation of a *digital portfolio*. This task consists of a compilation of reflections which draw from several elements, as we shall see, including personal professional experience, collegial work, and everyday professional practice. As a piece of work, it resides in a particular section of the college's VLE, the Moodle platform.

In my observation of Anne's assignment, I noticed that she chose to work on this task alone, separate from the rest of the class and in a workspace within one of the many pods facilitated by the Flexible Learning Centre. This is in contrast to Sara (Chapter 3) and Paulo (Chapter 5, to come), both of whom did not have the luxury of choosing where to do their writing. According to the assessment criteria, the digital portfolio is meant to be a collection of 'on-the-job' reflections and evaluations of 'naturally occurring' uses of technology in each learner's context. Since the learners in the course are themselves mostly teachers at the Woodale College, these contexts are primarily their own teaching environments. There is, therefore, a considerable level of freedom accorded to them in writing this assignment and, as we see in the vignette that follows, this proves a challenge for the tutor when it comes to designing and setting the task.

The tutor for the course, according to her own blog, has difficulty deciphering the course handbook's jargon when considering the assessment tasks for the course. The course has three units, and each unit has between 6 and 12 assessment criteria. Assignments need to meet these outcomes, with evidence required from 'naturally occurring workplace activity'. So tasks for assessment must provide the required evidence while the learner is 'on the job'. The tutor reflects as follows regarding the course handbook's instructions for assessment:

"I don't want to dictate to the students about how they should present their work—that's kind of the point of the course—they need to research, use and evaluate a range of technologies and find what suits them as individuals. Therefore, I think that this course is going to be a learning curve in terms of how collaborative technologies can be integrated with each other to provide a digital portfolio of evidence, but what that leaves me with this year is the potential for a lot of different systems to assess. Gulp!"

The phrases "naturally occurring workplace activity" and "on the job" clearly show that the digital portfolio is an individual matter for each course participant. Their own specific teaching contexts and reflective practices with digital media give rise to different sets of circumstances, insights, and problems, and therefore different accounts within their assignments. The tutor describes these as drawing from a range of "different systems". For her, this is an indication of the potential for variation across all the digital portfolios she receives and the difficulty this could bring for standardised marking and assessment. Different systems (blogs, web pages, contexts, etc.) will also bring a disparity of practices *within* one assignment for its writer, and we can see something like this from Anne as she commences her work.

Anne begins her assignment with an exclamation of excitement. She logs on by typing 'Posterous Spaces' (the blogging platform for learners on the course) and encounters the welcome screen which states, 'Posterous Spaces is the easiest way to share safely'. She clicks on 'Spaces', and then on 'Anne—TFLD'. These are her posts in draft form which she is currently working on and to which she will eventually link in her digital portfolio. She starts working on one of a number of blog posts which are in draft form, waiting to be uploaded for the world to read. She has been writing these over the last few days.

She uses the blog as part of her reflections for the course. It is the 'personal reflective' blog, and the first of two blogs she compiles. Selections of all these form parts of the digital portfolio. She shares this blog with four other learners in a group. The other, second blog, is the main course blog where all the learners of the TFLD course share things.

Then she clicks on 'Exactly how will I use the VLE with my students?' Another draft post is 'Face to Face or Facebook?' She chooses the first one and clicks on the icon that looks like an eye. Immediately after, she seems unsure as to what to do next (for a few seconds only) until she quickly clicks on the link again: a new tab opens.

Here Anne is mobilising different texts, each of which will, in various ways, influence her assignment. Before these aspects are looked at individually, it is important to get a better idea of how they come together through Anne's digital literacy practices, as a whole, and constitute her portfolio assignment.

Anne's digital portfolio assignment ends up consisting of a series of online reflections about her teaching practice and engagement with technologies for her teaching. These reflections are collected from a number of sources she has been working on before the assignment was even issued, through her *naturally occurring workplace activity*. These include a blog (see Figure 4.1) which she shares with four other students in the group, her own personal blog, a blog for the entire group, and her Twitter updates and Diigo links.

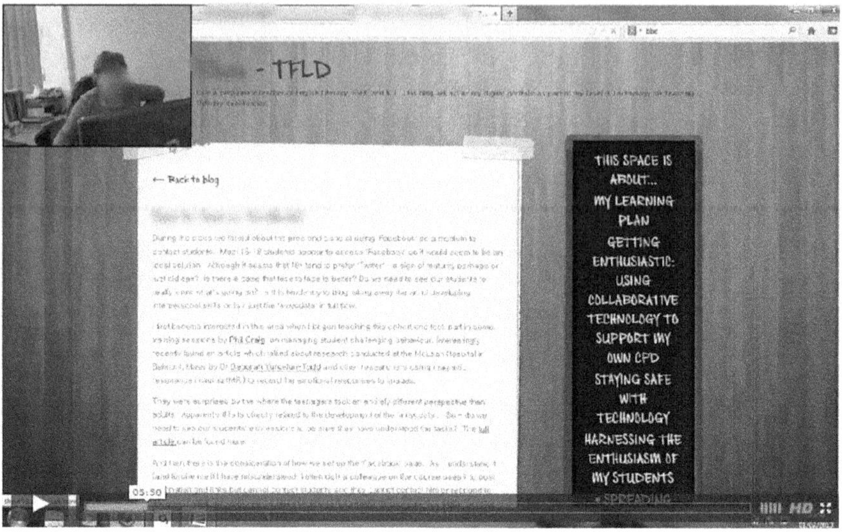

Figure 4.1 Screenshot of Anne Editing a Blog Post

These online reflections end up consisting of things such as the following:

- Her personal reflections on her *own* blog. These are usually posts where she writes about how she and her students (on the course she teaches) have responded to the use of a particular technology for learning and teaching as well as general posts about her professional life. *This is Anne as reflective teacher.*
- The selected tweets which she writes and posts at any time of the day and in any location via her mobile device. During the writing session, outlined next, she attempts to link her Twitter account with the blog and subsequently tweet blog updates through it. Anne uses Twitter only for professional discussions within networks of other college teachers. *This is Anne as networked professional.*
- Her posts and contributions on the course blog are open to all the other learners on the course. These blog posts can often be part of longer discussions with her classmates. Through this blog, she also comments on posts written by the other course participants. *This is Anne as collegial student.*
- Her Diigo[5] roll, which she embeds into a page within the VLE, as the college's ILT standards of practice stipulate, through which she provides links to web content for her students. *This is Anne as dutiful practitioner at Woodale College.*

These are overlapping assemblage identities upheld by their own sets of digital literacy practices. In each assemblage identity, Anne is positioned as a subject in a particular way: a reflective college professional, a collegial student, a subject of the college's ILT directives. Becoming a *subject* in this way, and the *hailing* that invokes and instigates it, is termed by Marxist philosopher Louis Althusser as "interpellation" (Althusser, 1977). Ideology is inculcated through the apparatuses of interpellations and their practices.

These assemblage identities form an important part of this analysis, and I will discuss them more depth later. But in the following vignette, we can see some of the practices which hold them together emerging within the assignment writing and subsequently holding that together too. Here Anne tweaks a previously written text to make it less critical and more suitable for her peers to read, and now the examiner of her digital portfolio has been added to the readership of the post.

Three minutes into the task, Anne is still editing a previously written blog post to include in her digital portfolio. She clicks on the option 'Edit' and adds the text 'VLE' before the word 'knowledge' in the text. She looks for another part to edit, and then she adds 'some of my' before the words 'immediate peers . . .' After looking at the screen for another 28 seconds, she saves the changes.

This editing seems to lessen the critical force of the text, which could be read as a slight criticism of her peers. This is tailoring the text for inclusion into her digital portfolio.

She refreshes the page, scrolls down, then up again, moves the page in a little more, and then clicks on 'Manage' followed by 'Drafts', and now she chooses the second of the options: 'Face to Face or Facebook?' This is a blog post about the pros and cons of using Facebook to communicate with her students. She clicks on the 'Edit' option again and then selects a name in the text ('Phil Craig'), chooses to 'Insert/Edit Link' (small window), but changes her mind and then cancels without editing/inserting anything. She then gives the text ('Face to Face or Facebook?') a cursory reading to check if it is OK and then clicks 'Publish'. She has just published a post on her blog which had until now been in her 'Drafts' folder and then links to it in her digital portfolio. This has direct implications for the assignment as an example of the kinds of 'signposting work' that she has to do for it: much of the digital portfolio will consist of links to her online reflections, posts, etc.

As she returns to the 'Posterous Spaces' tab, which is the service hosting her blog, she attempts to connect her Twitter account to the blog so that she can 'autopost' from it. This involves clicking on 'Manage'→'Autopost setup'→'Add a service'. This links her Twitter account to the blog and authorises 'Posterous Spaces' to send tweets announcing new posts. She needs to provide her username and password in order to achieve this authorisation. We are now ten minutes into the task.

Her strategy of collating—or curating[6]—a wide range of content which, in turn, link to other online content (e.g. her LinkedIn page) is Anne's strategy of addressing the unit criteria for the assignment. This is outlined by Anne herself in our discussion after the recording of the session when I asked her about this strategy, as shown in the following extract.

Anne: . . . It's where you pull together all the criteria and you say "this is how I meet it", but mostly directing to the posts on the blog. So that's why I'm jumping backwards and forwards . . . from my digital portfolio to the blogs, well both blogs, to the Internet, to Diigo, to Pinterest.
Ibrar: How long do you think the digital portfolio will be when you're done?
Anne: Around four pages with each page at around 400–800 words, with it all linking to things like posts and websites, and news reports and things like that. And that will cover all the criteria of the course.
Ibrar: So it's a piecemeal type completion isn't it?
Anne: Yeah it is; it is. You're doing bits of it.

Flows and the Blurring of Boundaries

In the recording of the session in which Anne works on her assignment, it is apparent that a wide range of digital environments, and her contributions and discussions in them, contribute to her digital portfolio as she sees fit. This is achieved through an abundance of hyperlinking: her response to the 'signposting' instruction as stated in the assessment criteria. But at the same time—and crucially—doing so causes Anne to rehash and fine-tune previous content to ensure its suitability for this new purpose.

Even though the content itself was written in different spatial and temporal locations, and for probably a different audience and other intentions in mind, this strategy for writing allows her to select from a wide pool of content for her digital portfolio. The agency of the digital portfolio, as an actant in this assemblage, eventually renders much of her online written work as professional or study related, even if it was not intended as such at the original time of its writing. This aspect was explored later in an interview in which Anne and I discussed her practices across home and work with the help of a Venn diagram, as shown in the extract that follows and aided by Figure 4.2. Following the mapping methodology, I advised that the diagram can be annotated and scribbled upon to show movements and 'flows' of her practices:

Ibrar: You also talked about how you use Twitter and LinkedIn.
Anne: Yeah and different people using it for different things. And for me, I have quite a clear delineation. As I said, I use them for different things, and for me that works. And I also don't like duplication. LinkedIn is my CV and Twitter tells me what's happening in education or technology. I don't go to silly sites. Facebook is usually for friends and family, but now the borders are being blurred as

> [professional] groups and things appear that seem interesting. So it's very difficult. So I use Pinterest to bookmark things that are of interest to me personally, so it may have pictures of my house on it [laugh]. Whereas I use Diigo to bookmark things that are professionally of interest to me, like sites for resources to use in the classroom.

Anne attempts to maintain a 'clear delineation' when it comes to digital media use for work, study, and home, and this is somewhat borne out more visually in the picture of her Venn diagram in Figure 4.2, which was taken as it was emerging during our discussion. The question of whether any web activities remain solely personal in her life is one I addressed in this discussion with her, and again to help us unpack this, the Venn diagram helped her to visualise the answer as she explained.

The Venn diagram shows a lot of activities initiated in the 'work' sphere which then flow into other domains of Anne's life, supporting the idea that technologies are introduced through work-based activities and initiatives, and then get picked up in other parts of her life. Notably, Anne mentions certain technologies that she would like to explore further and learn about, but she places the icons for these under the 'work' section, suggesting that it is most likely in her work activities that these new technologies are likely to be introduced and employed.

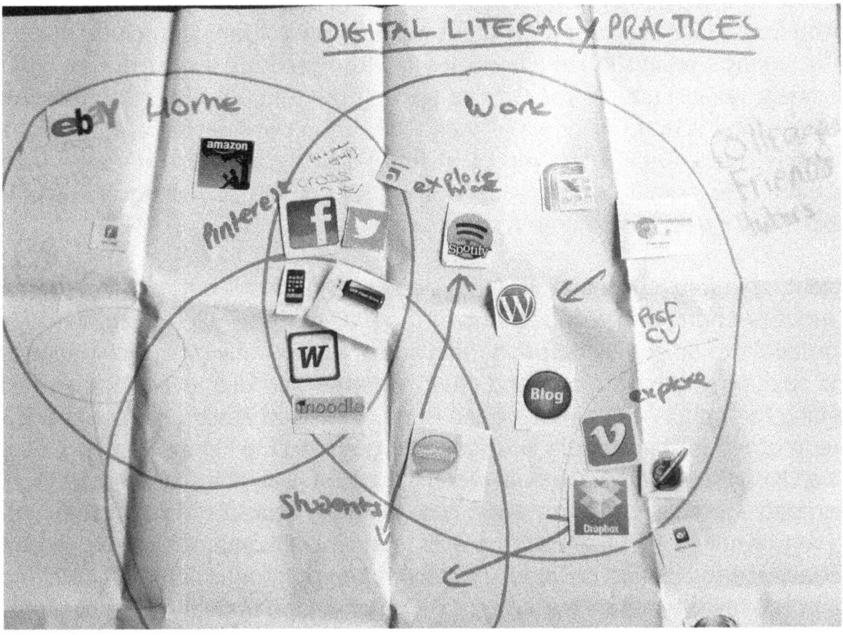

Figure 4.2 Anne's Venn Diagram of Digital Literacy Practices

The 'clear delineation' might be something she wishes to maintain, but with an assignment such as the digital portfolio designed the way it is (with instructions to continually 'signpost', etc.), we can envisage Anne's preferred practice of delineation to be challenged. The nature of the assignment demands some movement of her practices with digital literacy across her delineated contexts (work, home, etc.); they are better described as kinds of "boundary crossings"—a phrase that Ivanič and Satchwell (2007) deploy to describe literacy practices which crossover contexts. For Ivanič and Satchwell, the crossing is one of the interfaces between students' literacy practices in their lives beyond the classroom and institution, and into the different domains of their lives. They argue that the literacy practices taking place in these other domains, and their unique characteristics, can be a source of knowledge and learning which can, in turn, transform pedagogies and classroom practice.

These crossings are not without a subsequent transformation; as practices cross assemblage identities, they are transformed and their original purposes are betrayed, as Anne re-wrote texts to suit the criteria of the assignment. Instances in the recording of the assignment where this 'fine-tuning' or rehashing of previous content occur are further discussed in the next section, with more vignette extracts.

Rehashing Previous Work

In the following extracts, we return to Anne editing some text which she wrote previously, and for a different purpose. Her aim is to include this text in her digital portfolio, so her editing is about making it more aligned with the assignment task. At the time of writing the text, there was no intention of including it in a future assignment but, upon considering it appropriate, she fine-tunes some select pieces in line with her assignment's assessment criteria. The text is a brief reflection of how some of her peers have not responded positively to new technologies.

Twenty minutes into the task, Anne begins to navigate her way through the various sections and sub-sections of the VLE repository to get to her digital portfolio. Stored somewhere in its vast and complex network of web pages lies the specific page in which Anne must write her portfolio, even though much writing for it may have already been done, scattered across different parts of the Internet. In the Moodle interface she goes to 'My Home' tab → 'Course Overview Plus'→'Certificate in Technology in Learning Delivery'→'Digital Portfolio'. She is accessing the digital portfolio stored on the VLE in order to write within the VLE's interface and to actualise some of the links to other texts that she has just collated. This is the first point at which the actual digital portfolio is visible on the screen. Although all the textual work prior to this moment is indicative of it, and will connect to it, this is the portfolio.

She clicks on the link of the digital portfolio and enters its various subcategories. Its five assessed elements appear:

Learning plan
Getting enthusiastic: Using collaborative technology to support my own CPD
Staying safe with technology
Harnessing the enthusiasm of my students
Spreading the enthusiasm using the skills I have developed to support colleagues' use of technology in learning delivery

The practices of a) writing a text somewhere other than where the digital portfolio is stored but eventually linking to it and b) editing previously written texts for a new purpose have direct implications for the digital portfolio assignment and tell us much about Anne's strategy to address her task. A digital portfolio criterion mentions the importance of 'signposting work' and this is precisely what Anne spends 20 minutes preparing up to this point into the task. But another criterion mentions that the content should be 'current'.

The digital portfolio itself will not be a unified text which is submitted and stored as a single file such as the kind of assignment Sara had to complete; much of it will be linked to her online reflections and other elements she has drawn from. So the tweaking and fine-tuning by Anne of her blog post is necessary and meticulous. She values this online presence and wants to make sure that her digital portfolio is representative of her best online writing and professional activities.

Signposting

Only selected parts of these snippets of web-based writing end up as signposted to her digital portfolio, which is stored on the VLE. It remains a piece of work which is brought together by hyperlinks to the pieces of text to which she carefully chooses to link. The assignment for Anne, therefore, is the collection of these connections she is making and developing from *what is being written now, what has been written in other places and at other times, and what will be written in the future*. This is related to online activities she undertakes that are commensurate with her multiple identities and interpellating agencies: a *teacher* (writing things for the benefit of her students), a *student* (posting things for her tutor on the TFLD course and co-students on the course), and an aspiring *professional* (what she posts, more generally, about the UK college sector).

In the following vignette, we can see practices hailing from these assemblage identities being mobilised into this literacy event. These practices of signposting and linking from different elements are crucial to the assignment, and its fractal nature. These kinds of practices are further theorised in Chapters 7 and 8. The vignette shows that she often refers back to the criteria to decide whether a reflection is worthy of being included in the digital portfolio.

Forty minutes into the task, Anne still has the digital portfolio open on her screen in Moodle. She rereads the task instruction to 'signpost' and then connects with her Twitter account: she selects the word 'Twitter' from the text, and 'Insert/Edit link'. She embeds a link to her Twitter account.

She goes back to the 'Digital Portfolio' main page and then to 'Get enthusiastic . . . CPD' then 'Edit'. With the text she copied before (the text is still selected), she copies it again and tries to paste it in the 'HTML format' box in the 'Digital Portfolio' tab ('Edit' option). This is not working ('Copy/Cut/Paste is not available . . .'; small window appears).

She experiences difficulty copying and pasting when working with multiple tabs online. She repeats the process again (Copy/paste) and ends up with the same result as before. A window appears again, informing her about the problem, she clicks 'Cancel' this time. Copies the text again, and she copies it from Word this time—it works. She immediately saves her work.

The signposting and linking of elements in this way forms a key strategy of Anne's as she tries to avoid duplication of work and tries to draw from her own personal blog and personal social networking activity for her digital portfolio. This type of activity can be characteristically described as curation (see Chapter 6) and relates to how Anne selects, organises, and (re)presents content for her digital portfolio. Literacy events from the past and present, and their contents, are thereby curated by Anne for her assignment, and old texts are given new life. The digital portfolio itself is heavily curated rather than written up on a blank page 'from scratch'.

This is because the digital portfolio is a space, an environment, in which an assemblage is formed by Anne. Her selection of what to include—and what not to—is of note, as the digital portfolio is shaped by Anne's digital literacy practices. She seems readily able to mobilise and utilise content from various domains (work, study, and home), and integrate them into her digital portfolio. Yet the digital portfolio itself, in turn, influences Anne's overall practices with digital literacy in her out-of-college life with the kinds of boundary crossings discussed earlier.

Writing Through the Assessment Criteria

As the digital portfolio develops into a network of connections Anne has made, as a stand-alone document, it becomes quite short in length (c. 400–800 words) because of the links with other online texts and web pages. In addition to this, Anne employs another writing tactic. She also copies and pastes the criteria of the digital portfolio, the assessment rubric, directly and then writes her own text beneath it. Then she deletes the criteria which she earlier inserted. This is shown in the vignette that follows, which is drawn from the video log of her recording:

Anne then copies the text of the assessment criteria, pastes it into the text box meant for the digital portfolio, and then intersperses her own writing through it: a form of scaffolding, writing within writing. When asked about this later, she said it is because she has "a real problem with memory" [from the interview].

The text of the assessment criteria eventually becomes deleted as it is eaten up by her own writing, at which point she feels satisfied that she has addressed it enough in what she has written.

The text she writes is as follows:

To enable me to contribute to professional communities, I joined and set up a profile in 'twitter' and 'LinkedIn' several months ago. I initially set them up following discussions with peers and my tutor on the ADTELLS course last year but I did not really consider the content of my profile nor participate to any great extent. Although it is still relatively early in the Technology for Learning Delivery course, class discussions have led me to look at my profile on these sites and to consider more in depth my 'internet presence'.

Choosing a font becomes an issue, as does copying and pasting text across incompatible platforms such as from 'Word' to Moodle's 'HTML text editor'. Anne has to copy-paste it into notepad, then copy-paste it all again into Moodle.

Anne engages in this practice to ensure that she meets the criteria by having it right there in front of her as she types content for the digital portfolio. We see this 30 minutes into the recording, when the digital portfolio is visible for the first time on the screen via the Moodle interface (see Figure 4.3). Anne talks further about her strategy of copying and pasting the assessment criteria into the assignment and writing over it, in the discussion we had:

Anne: Also I have a real problem with memory, so what I tend to do is I have things like that [the criteria] so I'm cutting and pasting, and I can work my way through and say yep right OK for that, and then I delete it once I've written what I need to do about it. So it's kind of a reminder, rather than looking at different things and moving backwards and forwards—that doesn't work with me. But, subsequently, I have stopped doing this now, and the digital portfolio is much simpler than what it was as I link from it instead of writing lots.

Ibrar: You had problems copying and pasting into Moodle didn't you?

Anne: Yes, again these are just the foibles of jumping between things.

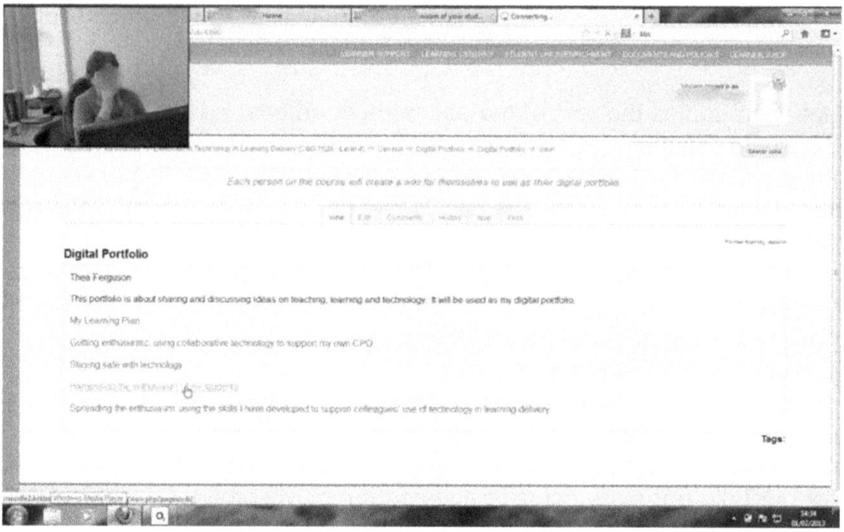

Figure 4.3 The Five Assessed Aspects and Sections of Anne's Digital Portfolio

The strategy of using the assessment criteria as a form of 'scaffolding' is one where Anne types through the words of the criteria and attempts to address its requirements, and then subsequently deletes it. Here Anne has forced a *recontextualisation* of the criteria, through her translation and interpretation of it, mediated easily by the digital media available at hand. In this vein, assessment criterion that must be adhered to is a powerful actor that has become transmitted across social boundaries via the dynamism of this assemblage. It forms the parameters within which Anne's assignment is to be judged with respect to how it meets the assessment criteria and course goals; it funnels her practices.

We can also view this as part of the 'life' of the assessment criteria as a literacy event in its own right. Here it serves a new purpose in a new situation as part of its textual trajectory. As this recontextualisation takes place, Anne adds and deletes elements of meaning, in her interpretation of it, and tries to address its dictates as part of the assignment task. This is an important moment in the chain of practices leading up to the completion of the assignment. In recontexualising the criteria, she attempts to carry their meanings whilst anticipating how they will be understood by the assessor who receives her work, all as part of her goal to complete the assignment as best she can.

What occurs in the earlier vignette and immediately following it shows a piecemeal completion of the digital portfolio assignment, with chunks of text reformulated from the criteria into reflections and links to other pieces of text. Anne copy-pastes the criteria for each of the five assessed aspects of the portfolio. Those aspects are shown in a screenshot (Figure 4.3) and reproduced here as follows:

1 My Learning Plan
2 Getting enthusiastic: use collaborative technology to support your own CPD
3 Staying safe with technology
4 Harnessing the enthusiasm of your students
5 Spread the enthusiasm: use the skills you have developed to support colleagues' use of technology in learning delivery

Slightly later on, nearly 50 minutes into the task, we see another clear example of Anne writing through the words of the criteria, using it as scaffolding for her own words in order to ensure that she is as close as possible to its requirements. Also, during this period, there are four tabs open in the browser, and she navigates across them drawing inspiration and ideas. She writes about the viability of the LinkedIn and Twitter platforms, and how they have supported knowledge development as part of her professional practice. This text, as we shall see next, eventually becomes incorporated into the digital portfolio as well.

The Foibles of Jumping

Anne multitasks extensively during her writing for this assignment. She repeatedly switches between tabs and programmes as she maintains a series of connected and concurrent tasks on the screen. Of course, as she operates on a single screen, only one task is foregrounded at one time. This multitasking is needed partly because the assessment criteria's injunction to 'signpost' demands it, and she can flick through the various tabs and windows with ease, but also (as substantiated in our interview) features as her strategy. But this is not always easily achievable.

The movement between tabs, web pages, and platforms does not always go smoothly, and Anne refers to this as the 'foibles of jumping between things' (see earlier interview extract). Choosing a font and copying and pasting text across incompatible platforms (from 'Word' to Moodle's HTML text editor) is problematic for her, as text from a website contains hidden formatting code embedded within it, which can be retained into the platform (here, Moodle HTML text editor) it is pasted into. The formatting code is a kind of hidden 'baggage' that is carried into the new context when it is copied and pasted. Web-based platforms are not always interoperable and apparently simple things such as web text can be loaded with hidden elements of code which may not be compatible with another platform (in this case, Moodle). Anne persists in trying to copy-paste into Moodle from her blog and eventually attempts what is otherwise a simple procedure via a basic word processor, and it is successful. Here the text and the software governing its arrangement and presentation in a web page are all part of the assemblage which then requires the mediation of another actor—a basic word processor—in order to insert text into a Moodle interface. An apparently simple procedure is made difficult, and it requires a creative and improvisatory 'workaround' by Anne and mobilisation of another actor along with some improvisatory digital literacy practices to achieve this.

Summary

As Anne writes her digital portfolio, we can see a host of interrelated elements being juggled and coordinated together. She manages to *recontextualise* previous texts, breathe new life into them and give them a new purpose. At times, this was merely a fine-tuning of something written at a different spatial and temporal location to the current event. On another occasion, it was her practice of writing through the assessment criteria as a type of scaffolding and adroit invoking of a text-editing tool as a workaround. Events of the past become implicated and enrolled as actors in this current event, as part of the sociomaterial assemblage. Past texts are brought in as powerful actors to shape and direct the current writing task. What happened previously is stored and used carefully as it represents a certain type of validation and relevance to the current task.

In exploring Anne's practices with digital literacy, we are drawn to the future too. Anne's ongoing Twitter account becomes linked to this task and is something which she employs exclusively for professional purposes. Digital literacy practices for Anne emerge through other events and practices in her life and are all linked through chains of associations. This does not always work out as Anne intends, especially when different digital platforms and browsers appear not to be compatible, and she has to manage the 'foibles of jumping'. But these instances require the mobilisation of other actors, which in turn make further digital literacy demands on Anne. These can be understood as tasks within tasks, or literacies nested within literacies, a notion explored in more depth in the Chapter 6. Other aspects of her work and similar instances in the other cases are explored in more detail in later chapters.

Her digital portfolio follows a piecemeal type of completion, with elements carefully selected, reworked if necessary, and incorporated as she negotiates their relevance with the assessment criteria. This means she can work on her assignment in almost any location and with any suitable device (smartphone, tablet, etc.) if necessary. Yet in our interview discussion, she insisted on a 'clear delineation' of work/study and home activities when it comes to her practices of digital literacy. In this way, her entire work is self-organised in her own environment, with her own tools, and using her own preferred practices.

As I became more familiar with Anne following this assignment task, I noticed how her appetite for blogging and reflecting online to her colleagues increased. During the course, she reflected and blogged after almost every lesson to evaluate how technologies were received by her students or utilised for her own study practices, and on other challenges such as plagiarism and copyright in digital environments. These ongoing reflections are an indication of her growing confidence with digital media as a professional college teacher, supported by her student and development activities on the course.

Notes

1 The college's real name has been changed for the purpose of this research.
2 For a detailed explanation of the levels of UK qualifications in the further education system see https://www.ucas.com/sites/default/files/2015-uk-qualifications.pdf.
3 According the English and Welsh qualifications system, at the time of the writing of this book, Level 4 is considered commensurate with a first year of a university degree (see https://upload.wikimedia.org/wikipedia/en/4/42/QCF_common_English_and_Welsh_qualifications.jpg).
4 These include the video log for the session alongside field notes.
5 Diigo is a social bookmarking tool that allows users to keep track of their favourite and most useful websites for sharing, reading later, or to keep up to date with several websites at once.
6 The notion of curation is explored further in relation to all the cases in Chapter 7.

5 Paulo's Report on Social Media

Background

Northdale College is just a few miles down the road from Woodale College (Chapter 3), and within the same borough of the region. It is part of a newly merged college campus which has its main campuses located in two busy adjoining towns. This particular site is situated within a complex multicultural milieu and has a student cohort that mirrors the ethnic mix of the local population. According to a quality inspection report, conducted prior to undertaking the research, the college's enrolments are mostly at the pre-university level and in the vocational areas of retail and enterprise, engineering and manufacture, and health and public services.

This college also has a substantial range of courses specifically for learners aged 16–18, with over 4,000 of such students enrolled. It is a strong provision for 16- to18-year-old learners, alongside recent improvements to the college's provision for ESOL. Both of these provisions have been aided by recent strategic ICT developments, and this was a key factor which lead me to this particular course as a third focus of inquiry for this book. This chapter presents an account of a student in a course which encompasses the overlapping investments of the college: 'ESOL and ICT'. In the following account, vignettes are gleaned from data sources such as field notes and video logs, alongside interview extracts towards the end of the chapter.

The Course

The course for this case study is an 'ESOL and ICT' course held at the college site. The student participant, Paulo, is undertaking the course at Level 1 in the UK Qualifications and Credit Framework.[1] In early fieldwork for the site, the programme was described by the tutor as being a 'bridging course', which means that its function is to prepare students who would typically be enrolled on an ESOL-only course for 'mainstream' education, alongside an embedded ICT vocational specialism. This bridging element is achieved by the learners having to undertake an exam at the end of the course. But the exam is a generic English language qualification that is not even designed for ESOL learners. This complicates things slightly and influences the tutor's methods and approaches to teaching the class because the mainstream qualification is considered to be more difficult—and unsuitable—for second-language speakers such as Paulo.

Additionally, the students are aged 16–18, and thereby fall into a category of people dubbed by some (e.g. Roberge *et al.*, 2009) as 'generation 1.5'. Roberge *et al.* (2009: 4) define this particular student group as "those who immigrate as young children and have life experiences that span two or more countries, cultures, and languages". The language-related needs of such a student group are problematised by some (e.g. Simpson *et al.*, 2008) as not neatly fitting into either a college's ESOL or literacy provision. Perhaps quite appropriately then, in the 'ESOL and ICT' course, the students are aspiring to join mainstream education upon successful completion of the generic English assessment and to be able to sit next to their native-speaking peers in the classroom rather than in a discrete ESOL programme.

According to a quality inspection report, immediately prior to the research, the college's ESOL provision yielded low attainment levels, unsatisfactory feedback, and major reforms to all aspects of the provision. Since the report, some progress has been achieved because of large-scale investments to the ESOL provision. According to the teacher of the ESOL and ICT course, some of these major revisions include increased utilisation of digital technologies in ESOL classrooms, assessment activities, and curricular topics. This is embodied in the title of the very course ('ESOL and ICT'). Further comments in the report highlight access to ICT resources as satisfactory with accessibility issues such as slow network speed significantly hindering students' work, particularly when they attempt to log in simultaneously. This is something that was also borne out in my observation of the classes and during Paulo's assignment, discussed next.

At the term's end, the teacher conducted an interesting experiment for the class. She got the students to evaluate the different technologies they had used throughout the duration of the term. Using a web-based student response system known as 'Socrative', she presented a number of multiple choice and short answer questions to which the students responded via their preferred choice of mobile device (personal or college owned). Students had the option to log on via their iPads, mobile devices, laptops, or classroom desktops in order to take part. To her surprise, the 'best' or 'favourite' choices of technologies used by the students were not the ones she had anticipated or regularly utilised as part of teaching.

This process by the tutor is an important planning tool for future cohorts of the course, especially as the programme will be benefitted by college-wide enhancements such as improved Wi-Fi and a new Open Learning area (see Figure 5.1) where students are encouraged to use their mobile devices more effectively. This kind of freedom of Internet access brings with it a host of other issues when it comes to planning learning activities, designing assignments, and even organising the timetable as activities and events are *reassembled* with new digital practices. The Open Learning area is part of a new

Figure 5.1 The Open Learning Area of Northdale College Encourages Students to Use Their Own Devices

investment, but its impact has not yet been felt, especially for courses such as Paulo's, which require a great deal of teacher supervision. Paulo remains confined to a musty classroom for most of his sessions—a room stuffed with digital investments from the previous tranche of college funds. This is demonstrated in the following vignette, which is drawn from observations of a class.

This is the first session of the course. I notice that the room is arranged in four rows of desks with PCs for each person along the row. This makes it awkward to get from one side of the room to the other. I had to squeeze behind students sitting at their desks to find a place sit down. The age of the building suggests that the room was not designed for its current computer-intensive activity. Being full of equipment, the room is always locked and even the teacher requires a key to access it for her lesson. She has to get this key from a designated person, an 'IT guy'. This results in a moment of panic immediately before the lesson, as the IT guy is not in his office. PCs make the desk arrangement more individual, the room less accessible, and give the place a musty smell.

The individualised desk arrangement means that during the lesson, the teacher has to go around to the different desk spaces regularly and mediate her instructions alongside machine and web-based interaction. She doesn't mention the college's new Open Learning Centre.

Most of the classrooms in the college require a key to access them, and this is usually held at a central staff location or carried by a member of staff who will regularly use the room. On the occasion of an observation, as noted earlier, the key was held by an individual who was not immediately available at the start of the lesson, resulting in a moment of panic. The unique nature of the room, being full of expensive digital investments results in a limitation of free and open access for staff and students alike. The instance here of a locked room causing delay tells us something about forms of access and barriers we see Paulo, his teacher, and his classmates facing during the assignment-writing process. Locks and barriers of all sorts are set up and held in place by an ICT-intensive administration at the college, which serves to keep a certain type of 'assemblage' in order. This ICT administration promotes and upholds throughout the college a culture of data storage, digital communications for staff and students, decision making, and record keeping (among other things). Its focus is primarily on ICT for managerial efficiency and effectiveness, like many administration systems in modern educational contexts (Ghavifekr *et al.*, 2013).

Double Intention

The purpose of the work prior to the assignment was for the students to design and complete a small survey to explore their opinions of using social media sites for educational purposes. This was achieved through a questionnaire which examined their 'pros and cons', and served as foundational work for the following week's assignment on the topic. The brief of this assignment was handed out by the teacher at the end of the lesson. The exact text is reproduced in the following text box with its formatting retained.

The assignment brief clearly delineates the wishes of the tutor in how she would like this assignment to be completed. The brief serves a dual purpose and reflects the *double intention* of the course (ESOL and ICT): i) to outline the topic of the task (ICT) and ii) to outline the language features required for the task (ESOL). She has conveniently typed the latter in italics (e.g. *use sequence markers*). At a later date, in a lesson following this one, I recorded Paulo's assignment being written, as he drew guidance from a number of sources including this very hand out, a previous week's survey data, the teacher's notes on the board, and guidance as laid out in the college VLE.

We now come to the session in which Paulo handles the assignment. Ahead of him stretches one and a half hours, during which he must complete his class project. His task was to create a spreadsheet of the survey results of the benefits of different social media platforms and to discuss the results in a report. The following vignette account is drawn from the video logs for Paulo's recording together with field notes. The purpose of the lesson was to

Homework

Write a report about Social Networking.
5 paragraphs.
Introduction

- What the report is about
- What I will write about
- *Use sequence markers*

The Pros and Cons comparing 4 networking sites (Facebook, U-tube, Twitter, College VLE)
Use Comparatives and Superlatives
Class survey on social networking results

Use Adverbs of Frequency

- 7 people blog daily, 3 weekly, 2 less than that
- 1 person uses 9 social networks 1 person uses use only 1 blog and 2 people don't have a blog
- Most people use blogs for chat fun, to send pictures and video, and to share information
- 8 people use English to blog, no one uses only mother tongue, and nine people use both

How I use social networking

Use Adjectives

Conclusion—My opinion on social networking.

Use Opinion Phrases

Figure 5.2 The Text of the Homework Handout Given to Paulo

complete the report which outlined the pros and cons of social networking sites for educational purposes.

As the session begins, the teacher has problems accessing the correct link as she tries to open up the relevant file to display assignment instructions on the interactive board. An ICT technician is called in and arrives within five minutes to remedy the situation, and a display of the assignment's instructions becomes visible on the board. But his work does not end there: There is a problem accessing the college's VLE (Moodle) platform to gain access to further task instructions and supporting resources which the teacher has collated for the students to help them with this particular task. Meanwhile, the teacher is going around the room reminding and clarifying the structure of this assignment, its language features, paragraphing, etc., while addressing both the entire class and individual students with variations of the same instructions. This is a big deal for her; she mentions them repeatedly throughout the session.

The report which the students have to write uses data from a class survey which was the last lesson's homework. The teacher keeps reminding—even pushing—the students to access the 'Diigo roll'[2] to find links with the relevant information to help with the assignment. Diigo is a web bookmarking tool, which allows her to select and organise web links as resources to then share with her students via the VLE: a kind of 'curation'. She mentions this many times throughout the duration of the class, as we shall see later. The students are meant to use the links to then, in turn, search for further information themselves.

The nature of the course, particularly its ICT inflection, influences how the teacher conducts the class and administers the assignment. As a matter of protocol, she makes the students access course and assignment-related material via the VLE and makes a point that this is a part of the process of actually doing the assignment. She could initiate the instructions with handouts (in fact, she does later when things go awry), or display them on the interactive whiteboard (which she also does, but also later). But in the first instance, and to emphasise the 'ICT' part of this course, she sets a certain procedure in place—a modus operandi to get things done.

Instructions have been put into the VLE by the teacher for Paulo to access along with a list of links using Diigo. These are like 'hoops' for Paulo to 'jump through' as part of the task. The teacher could have just given them to Paulo, but, as we shall see later, she is under her own instructions to use technologies a certain way in her teaching and feels that she has to get students to obtain information in a certain way. It appears that she has her own hoops to jump through.

Hoops to Jump Through

To get a better idea of the hoops that the teacher has to jump through and the origins of why she feels the need to get the students to obtain information a certain way, we can take a look at the college's digital learning standards document. This document divides the use of digital media for learning and teaching into three levels of quality (bronze, silver, and gold) and is used as a basis for judging the quality of ICT adoption in lessons during inspections and quality assurance processes. An extract of text from the document is shown in Figure 5.3. Importantly, the standards document draws from guidelines set out in two other important strategic documents of the college: the "Strategic Vision" and the "Vision for Learning" documents. They are

Digital Learning Standards

This document defines a set of standards which are intended to improve student opportunities for learning. The purpose of this specification is to define a set of broad goals for course teams to aim to achieve. The standards should not be seen as rigid or definitive, there is an expectation that different course programmes will require different emphasis in particular areas. For example, there would be an expectation that a language course would have a greater use of communications tools.

Bronze *defines a set of core course resources that should be available in every course, allowing learners to understand the learning and assessment requirements of the course and to catch up on any missed sessions.*

Silver *is intended to allow students check their learning progress.*

Gold *provides independent learning opportunities not constrained by time or place.*

Bronze

Access to key course documents and core learning resources:

Requirement	Evidence
The course programme of study is available in the VLE, including overviews of the study modules/units with assessment requirements. The VLE course is organised and has a weeks or topic structure which maps to the session delivery programme. Comprehensive learning resource collection includes lesson handouts, slide presentations, video clips, animations and web links. Students actively use the VLE for resources and information. The majority of class resources are accessed and presented in class from the VLE. This helps learners because they see the tutor access the resources from the VLE during each lesson. Classroom-based learning is delivered using interactive whiteboard activities helping to keep learning fun and engaging. Students reflect and plan their own learning in the College eILP system. VLE course news forum used for notices to students. Assignment work support is available online from the VLE. A summary of module/unit learning.	A cut down and reformatted version of the scheme of work. The course is organised to reflect the scheme, making it easy for staff and students to find documents and information. Learning resources The VLE 'Participants' button to show students are logging on regularly, throughout the year. The VLE 'Participants' button shows that teaching staff regularly login to present class resources from the VLE. Lesson observation reports Resources available in the VLE Students using the new eILP system Forums used for course specific information/notices and discussions Assignment briefs, additional guidance and learning resources to support assignment work A completed Course Summary (including key words) to enable course searching.

Figure 5.3 Digital Learning Standards Document Extract

issued to every member of the teaching staff in both paper-based and electronic forms, and they are used as part of lesson observation and inspection activities. The directives of these documents are fresh in the teacher's mind, as she had faced an inspection during the period of my fieldwork, but not on a day that I was scheduled to visit the class.

The teacher's insistence on using the VLE to organise assignment tasks and related content shows how diligently she intends to adhere to the digital learning guidelines. And even her *own* enthusiasm for technology and web-mediated teaching emerges through the college's advised procedure. For example, the use of Diigo, for selecting and organising web links, is only because it is her preferred tool, but it must be embedded in the VLE for students to access. She therefore sets lots of 'tasks within tasks' in this way. Naturally, the assignment being about social networking makes this apparently ideal supplementary activity. But according to the criteria as set out in the digital learning standards document (see extract in Figure 5.3), to achieve a mere 'bronze' level of ICT use, a teacher at Northdale College must ensure the following:

- Students actively use the VLE for resources and information.
- They access the resources from the VLE during each lesson.
- Assignment work support is available online from the VLE.

The use of a VLE at this level is as a repository of course and assignment-related documentation and resources, and only at the 'higher' levels (silver and gold) is the VLE to be used as an interactive tool which provides instant assessment feedback and allows the learners to access learning and assessment material with minimal space and time restrictions.

As Paulo finally begins his work (see the following vignette), we see more instances of the teacher's insistence on the VLE, and this actually recurs throughout the task. This is shown in the vignette account.

As Paulo begins his assignment, he looks confused and deeply in thought; he frowns. He looks at the whiteboard, which has instructions for the task. He then looks down at a piece of paper, which also has instructions but with slightly different wording and focus to them. Earlier, the teacher had explained, verbally, the same instructions, thus catering to at least two learning styles: aural and visual. All these sources are actants that he must contend with. There is the whirring of the desktop units and the voices of the students discussing ideas and other, apparently unrelated, things. Momentarily, his frown lifts as he begins writing his assignment but he has—upon the teacher's insistence—had to login to the VLE to get more information on what to do: yet another actant. He acquiesces but with visible disapproval.

As he reaches the VLE interface to get to his work, he clicks on 'Participants' under the 'My Course: 15–18's ESOL research' option and then he seems unsure for a while about what to do next, until he decides to go back to '15–18's ESOL research'. At this point, he buttonholes the ICT support person, who is already in the room and is also getting others logged on to the VLE, as they seem to be having the same problem. He helps Paulo get to the right part of the VLE for his work. The ICT support person tells Paulo that he needs an 'enrolment key' for the course to gain access to the relevant page of the VLE for his task: yet another actant to contend with—a 'hurdle' designed by software engineers and implemented by an ICT-intensive administrative process.

In the vignette, Paulo still looked confused, despite the multiplicity of instructional sources, or perhaps because of them. But his frown momentarily lifted as he began writing his assignment. This was followed by a reiteration of the teacher's instruction to work via the VLE and to use it for information and resources. This information, and the resources, had been uploaded by the teacher and were meant to direct the content of the assignments for all the students, making sure that there was some equivalence of work across all of them. But in so doing, Paulo needed the help of an ICT support person to get access to the right part of the VLE. We also see the need here for another kind of 'key' (an enrolment key: a number to be inputted), which in turn will open another kind of 'door' (a web page) to Paulo where he needs to be to start his work. This, much like the key to access the room at the start of a lesson, causes a small amount of delay and frustration and requires a designated person to enter the scene to resolve the problem. That person belongs to the same ICT administrative team which held the keys to the door of the room.

There are two salient issues which emerge at this very early stage of the assignment: i) the need for 'keys' to access blocked areas, more of which we shall see later, and ii) the insistence of VLE integration at almost every stage of the assignment, more of which we shall also see later as Paulo gets on with his work. All these elements are actants for Paulo to contend with, and their involvement comes from a range of agencies and forces within and beyond the college to shape the agenda ahead of him, his teacher, and the assignment.

The digital learning standards dictate specifically how the teacher should use the VLE in the classroom. The standards shape a particular type of regime which is backed up by a cadre of the college's ICT administration who hold the keys (both physical and digital) to access spaces (also physical and digital in nature). The college is so invested in this ICT administration that staff professional development courses are full of training and guidance on utilising institutional platforms (such as the VLE) as part of what is deems as 'good practice'. The policies and training regime for staff originate from such things as the college's strategic vision and vision for learning documents, as well as improvements demanded in a recent inspection report (discussed at the start of the chapter). These agencies are meant to lead to a particular type of assignment product for Paulo at the end—an assignment whose content is drawn from pre-selected and curated resources by the teacher and placed within the password-protected VLE to attain a certain level of equivalence across all the students' work. But this knock-on effect is not without gaps, disjunctures, and non-coherences of actors. We can see these as chains of associations that attempt—or come close to providing—a stable assemblage through which assignment processes become entrenched in unacknowledged steps, alignments that are not always aligned, and connections that are sometimes tenuous or unreliable. Power and influence, therefore, are not intrinsic to a human or non-human actor, but a result of the relations; it may, therefore, need to be overcome or circumvented by the *irruption* (see Chapter 8) of new actors and the practices that come with them.

Disobedient Technology

New digital tools, ICT investments, more connectivity, differently designed assignments, etc., all bring differing alliances and assemblages, as well as new ways of doing student work. Forgetting the key to the door, forgetting one's password, or seeking out the person responsible for them demonstrates a system in which actors may not be aligned strongly enough in their various connections. Actors such as policies, which hail from such things as strategic visions, are written for particular types of alignments of people and things, and these may not travel well when new scenarios with new actors are involved, as we see in the next vignette, which is drawn from the video log data and field notes:

> Six minutes into the task, things are not cohering and no meaningful task engagement has occurred yet. The teacher seems a little frustrated because of the delay and confusion, as does Paulo, and even the ICT support person. In the meantime, a student has to leave the class in order to find the person who can provide him with his password. While waiting for that, the teacher tells everyone to work on their reports. Paulo goes back to Microsoft Word and starts typing again: "In my report . . ." He looks at the paper with his notes for a second that he now places in front of his keyboard and goes on typing. Meanwhile, the teacher gently chastises a student who has no survey results to work from, as he was absent yesterday. A chaotic classroom.

Immediately prior to this, Paulo was waiting for instructions, experiencing a loss of attention, and for a short period of time he was not connected to the task in any meaningful way. The teacher was getting frustrated by this delay and confusion; this was not helped by the fact that a student then had to leave the classroom to find the person who could give him his password to log on to the VLE. The need for a password is another obstacle which causes a small amount of disruption, just like the keys to the room and enrolment key before it.

We can view these as instances where some sociomaterial actants do not wish to cohere or work according to the script set for them in such things as the teacher's plan for the lesson. Their disobedience renders further actors (such as the ICT support person) to 'irrupt' (see Chapter 7) into action to maintain the apparent coherence of the dramaturgy of formal learning. When this entrance of the ICT support person causes a delay, Paulo senses frustration from all sides: from the teacher, the ICT support person, and himself. This ultimately impacts on how efficiently he facilitates his workflow from this point onwards in the assignment, as it finally gets underway. Not only Paulo but also the workflow of the teacher and the entire group is disrupted by this and the other student's password difficulty.

We can turn to Latour's fictional account of the failed technology of Aramis (Latour, 1996) to understand how a technology can be 'disobedient' or 'disloyal' to the interests of humans by a search for the "dismemberers of assemblages of humans and non-humans" (p. 74). A technology, Latour argues, does not fail (or act disobediently) because of a particular actor's inherent failing, but rather because of a multitude of actors' failures to sustain interdependence and "sociotechnical compromise" (p. 101). In his account of Aramis, inefficiency of the initiative and subsequent failure were caused by the number of actors not envisaged at the beginning of the innovation project which also then failed to cohere in any meaningful way. Latour argues that Aramis as a system failed not because of any one particular actor, but rather because the actors as a whole failed to sustain the project's overall aims through negotiation and adaptation.

This can also be the case with Woodale College's insistence on applying the Moodle VLE as a repository and facilitator of assignment tasks for all staff and students. But as a force, the managerial diktat (via policy documents, etc.) is not enough. A series of weighty actors need to hold the system steady (password-protected web pages, etc.), resulting in a tension of *incorporation* where the dominant system engenders compliance from subordinates and *excorporation* where subordinates appropriate the resources and commodities provided by the dominant system for their *own* practices (Fiske, 2011).

How Paulo copes with this kind of tension emerges throughout his writing for the assignment and is characteristic in the following vignette drawn from the video logs:

Ten minutes of the class have now elapsed. Paulo switches windows from Moodle to Microsoft Word, which contains his report, and alternately types and looks at his notes. He has to go back and forth across different web pages and his Word file, which has received little attention thus far, as he has spent the last few minutes merely getting organised and figuring out what to do. When he does get into the flow of writing, he receives an interruption: he is asked to return to the web page in the VLE. He scrolls down and clicks on 'Homework 12–02–2013 Social Networking Report' to download the file (right click—'Show in Folder'), and then he drags it onto his desktop. He opens the file and then goes back to his report and continues typing. The teacher directs everyone to look at the extra information on the board, which lays out the paragraphs for the report that are worded as follows on the slide:

Paragraph 1: Introduction, what I will write about
Paragraph 2: The pros and cons, comparing four networking sites
Paragraph 3: Class survey on social networking results
Paragraph 4: How I use social networking
Paragraph 5: Conclusion

Paulo then focuses on the look of the page, tweaking its layout (margins, font, etc.) as he types. This lasts into the twelfth minute. Whilst writing his report, he looks at his notes, pauses momentarily, and then writes about how Facebook, Twitter, and YouTube are the most popular social networks. He does this continuously.

Meanwhile, the teacher is heard in the background giving instructions, reminding students of what is required. Paulo is looking at his notes the whole time while typing. Spell checker interrupts often; he acquiesces, but one of such 'corrections' leads to another mistake, albeit not a spelling-related one.

In the vignette, Paulo referred to the 'Homework' file to check if he was doing things right and to see what to do next. He then went back to his report and started a new (third) paragraph, which opened with, "In my opinion", since he has been instructed to use opinion phrases (as stated in the homework file he had just consulted). The interruption he then received was about the paragraphing for the assignment (see Figure 5.4). This aspect

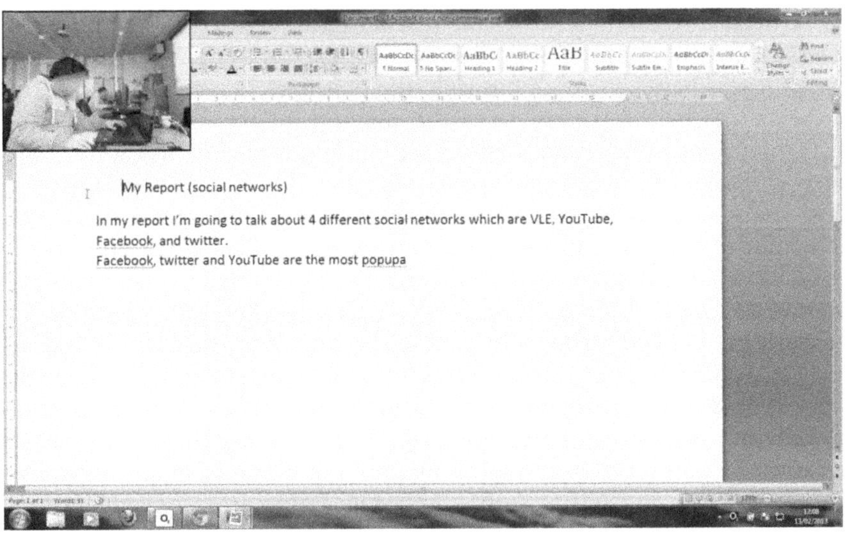

Figure 5.4 Screenshot of Paulo Trying to Shape His Work According to the Structure Set for Him

is connected to the English language agenda attached to the course and the looming exam facing Paulo, which causes concern for the teacher and most probably Paulo too. At this point, the language assessment, as interpreted by the teacher, became a key actant and was key in influencing and shaping his work. He was perhaps also thinking about grades, his parents' expectations, and his future career.

In the vignette that follows, and still early on in the assignment, Paulo had another interruption: this time by the teacher who asked him to follow the rubric and correctly format his document before starting the word processing assignment:

Twenty-five minutes into the task, the teacher stresses the format of the report and its structure, again! In response to the teacher feedback, Paulo edits his report. He writes "Introduction" above his first paragraph. He highlights it and puts it in bold and italics: *Introduction*. The teacher also reminds him about more things he needs to consider in his report (e.g. the differences and similarities between the various social networks) and how he must draw inferences from the spreadsheet. At this point, his introduction is only one line and a half, whereas his second paragraph is very long. The teacher also tells him about the kinds of comparison he could make—or should be making—as part of this task. What he had written prior to the teacher's intervention is now being shuffled into sections and labelled as 'paragraph 2, paragraph 3', 'conclusion', etc.

This was another interruption, and there were more to follow, in which the teacher re-reminded Paulo of the kind of writing he needed to do and how he needed to do it. Whether the teacher had weighed up the options of allowing Paulo to continue and then correct his work later, or whether she felt that it was better to get things right the first time, is not known. But this represents another vital element of this assignment scenario: lots of small tasks and instructions nested within a greater and more important task, in a *Matryoshka-doll*-type relationship (see Chapter 6).

The main task to be completed here was, of course, the assignment. But within it were nested many other tasks which Paulo was continually reminded about and each of which also required a certain level of capability: scanning the Diigo link roll for readings, addressing the language and grammar elements explicit in the rubric, etc. Some of these 'tasks within tasks' were less explicit and part of the dramaturgy of formal learning, such as the skills required to navigate around the pages of the VLE, interpreting different types of assignment instructions, etc. The work for these nested tasks was instantiated by different digital literacy practices. In many ways, this class assignment can itself be seen as an event within greater events beyond it—as part of other assemblages at different times and locations: a collateral reality (c.f. Law, 2012) in the life history of Paulo. Perhaps an incidental product, perhaps to be forgotten in later years, but nevertheless necessary for Paulo's future life and career. This assemblage became even more complex in the next vignette, where Paulo mobilised other actors for help:

Half an hour has now passed since writing commenced. As this is a language-related task (ICT and ESOL), Paulo has to use 'adverbs of frequency' (often, sometimes, rarely, etc.) in this assignment; this is explicitly stated in the assignment outline and stressed by the teacher. Paulo sprinkles these into his report. He then turns to Google—another actant which mobilised into the assemblage. He ends paragraph 3 and saves his report (again), closes both his files, and looks up at the board and around the room. After sitting silently for a few seconds, he then types 'social network' into the search bar. He selects 'Social Networking Service—Wikipedia', reads the text, scales the menu, and then Google Portuguese (www.google.pt); he types in Portuguese: 'redes sociais percentagens' [trans. social networks percentages] and visits the sites Google suggests. This is followed by another search: 'redes sociais mundo' [trans. social networks world]. He then clicks on the first site that appears in the list and takes a look. Followed by 'lingua redes sociasi' [trans. language social networks]. He reads a related article he finds now (in Portuguese and about Facebook). Meanwhile, the teacher reminds the class about how to use comparatives in the report.

The teacher wants the students to utilise the resources on the 'Diigo roll' which she has prepared in a page of the VLE. This is a list of links to supportive resources which she has uploaded onto the VLE so that the students do not have to randomly search the web for information and potentially write something that is not appropriate for the task. The Diigo roll makes sure they all have access to more or less the same set of content for the assignment. Paulo accesses it, and the Diigo link has not worked, but Paulo has already been hunting for information through Google on his own.

In the account, we see Paulo going about his assignment in a way he saw most appropriate for himself, even using his first language to aid him during Google searching. The instructions and directions to do things 'properly' persist. Paulo heard and saw all of this, yet quite perfunctorily continued on his path. His and the teacher's immediate goals always remained the same: the completion of the assignment.

The teacher then opened up the previous lesson's work, and its contents were utilised, especially the formatting and numerical data aspects of it. Extra 'help' was put on the board through a breakdown of the writing project's paragraphs, as suggested by the teacher, who again directed everyone's attention to the board: *Paragraph 1, Paragraph 2 . . .. Paragraph 5, Conclusion.* As Paulo transferred the contents of his notes onto the screen, the teacher approached him to monitor his work activities (see Figure 5.5). At this point, Paulo interfaced with various actants; there was a juggling of

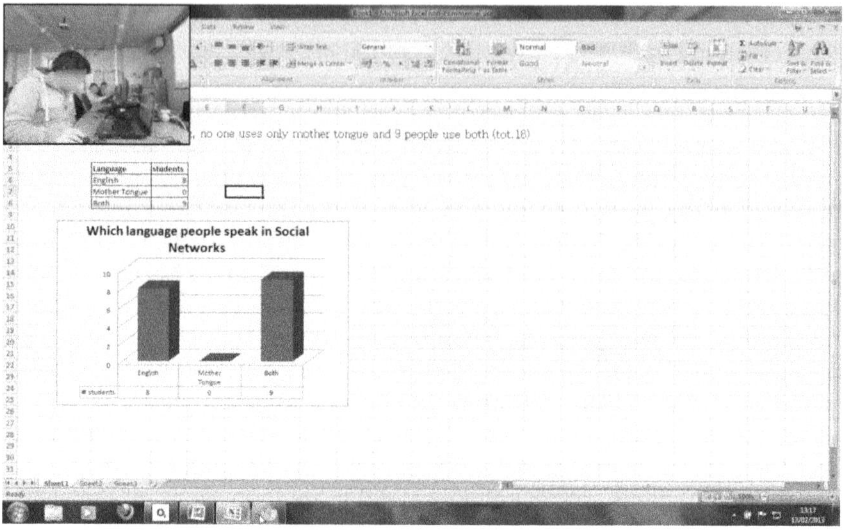

Figure 5.5 Paulo Incorporates a Graph from a Spreadsheet Into His Assignment, With the Help of the Teacher

several elements in getting the assignment done. This is another instance of the kind of Matryoshka-doll nesting of tasks:

1. His notes from a) the last session and b) added to in the current session.
2. The survey data from the previous lesson, which he interprets in the discursive text of his report (see Figure 5.5).
3. The content on the board.
4. The teacher's verbal instruction a) to the class, b) to him specifically, c) related to the language conventions of the task (paragraphing and coherence), and d) related to the topic of social networking.
5. Comments from classmates.
6. The task's written instructions from the VLE.
7. The formatting and tweaking of the page (margins, font, etc.) on screen.
8. The constant interruptions by spell checker's red lines (one such "correction" in fact selects the wrong word).
9. The web search results (Portuguese and English).
10. The writing/composing strategies of sentence-by-sentence (or word-by-word) revision or editing.
11. Paulo's prior experience and knowledge regarding classroom and assignment protocol. But also his expertise with a) cross-platform computer work (Excel to Word, Moodle etc.), and b) his choice of social networks to discuss for the assignment (related to his personal learner profile).
12. The ICT support person who enters to manage Paulo's VLE login problems.

The list highlights some of the agential forces woven in this complex and unfolding assemblage. Some of these forces are 'set up' by the formal learning environment and literacy practices associated with it (such as the teacher's formal instructions), others are capricious and off the cuff (such as comments from classmates), and others are unexpected or because of something 'not going as planned' (such as the needed intervention of the ICT support person). All of these factors required a judicious negotiation as Paulo wrote his assignment, created a chart, incorporated it, wrote about how the social networks are useful for him as a student, and finally submitted his work both *despite* and *because* of their involvement. His multitasking was remarkable, even though he probably felt as though he was floundering at the start.

In Figure 5.5, we can see Paulo's chart in Excel. In the following vignette, we see how Paulo struggled with this and how he was directed to a screencast to help him create this visual from numerical data and then import it into Word for his report:

An hour has now passed. Paulo is trying to create a chart. He chooses a 'column' amongst the options he is given. The column appears ('Students') with percentages (language students use). He tries out different styles for his column. This leads him to struggle when working across Word and Excel, as he figures out what to do in order to design the table (in Excel) and then create a graph for use in the report by transferring data from the 'homework' file, to the Excel table, to a graph, and then to discuss this in the report.

In order for Paulo to complete his assignment the way the teacher instructs, he has to access a video screencast (or screen recording) via the VLE (again!) which demonstrates how to make graphs and charts from numerical data entered into Excel. The screencast tutorial outlines how to make graphs and charts from numerical data entered into Excel. The teacher does this for him, whilst talking him through it. She directs him and the rest of the class to the help (for the project) she had already placed on the VLE for them to access in order to complete the assignment. It was there, just not organised clearly enough for Paulo to navigate his way through the pages easily enough to see it. But the Java plugin to play the screencast is not working. Paulo asks for help from the teacher with the site; she then takes the mouse from his hand and actually does it herself whilst explaining it to him.

At this stage, Paulo needed to incorporate some Excel data into his report, but this required making a graph, the procedure for which was outlined in a video tutorial he had to watch. The tutorial itself, however, could only work with a Java plugin installed on the machine—which then failed to work. The teacher then took the mouse off him and did it for him, whilst also explaining it to him as she did it. This shows that she was intent on sticking to her 'plan' for the lesson (including telling Paulo how to handle the video) and not allow non-cohering actants to get in the way of her instructional agenda.

As the session draws to a close, Paulo must submit his work. Again, a certain procedure was required in order to complete this, but again, Paulo did it his own way.

The lesson is coming to an end, and we are now at a crucial part of the assignment: its submission procedure. For the final part of his assignment, Paulo must upload his work to the VLE. This is the only way it can be submitted, and the teacher does not allow the students to email it as an attachment. Yet she receives several simultaneous requests for clarification on saving the assignment and uploading it to the VLE. All these voices represent their own complex assemblages of concerned student stakeholders, managers' directives and procedures, and employee protocol. The teacher says, "You need to save it in your library in the VLE, not your SkyDrive. For some reason, they are not interlinking, so you need to save your work to the VLE. And please don't save it in your email".

Paulo spends a couple of minutes going through the different options to find the section where he should submit his file. Finally, he decides to save it by sending himself an email with the report and graphic as an attachment. Then he uploads it as he should, as well as sending the email to himself. The teacher chastises a student for leaning back in his chair and instructs the students to reflect on this task in their blogs.

Paulo reflects in his class blog at the end about this assignment:

"I didn't learn new work but I learnt more things about Excel. I think it was interesting. Today, I was a bit confused but I think I did it well."

Given the multiplicity and competing agendas of all the actants at work; given the complexity of all their networks, visible and invisible; given that all neat pieces of work, course assignments, and all ordered systems result from messy beginnings, I too think he has done very well!

Here, again, the VLE emerged as a focal point, this time to direct the submission process. Despite the instruction to submit his work via the VLE, Paulo emailed the document to himself, contravening the teacher's instructions, but then attempted to submit it via the VLE as well just to be on the safe side. This is yet another, and final, instance where the 'doing' of the assignment has other tasks nested within it. And again, this is via the structuring agency of the digital learning policy of the college. Yet some of these nested tasks are supererogatory and done as a matter of course rather than as a necessary part of the assignment's actual completion: the dramaturgy of formal learning.

Interview Extracts

In this section, I will further explore the kinds of themes which emerged in my discussion with Paulo about his digital literacy practices across the domains of work, college, and home, as well as to help elucidate some of Paulo's assignment-related writing activities during the recording. When asked to recap on how he wrote the assignment and the kind of research he undertook and background knowledge he used to complete it, Paulo confirmed as follows:

Paulo: I went to the Internet and I've searched what they [social networks] are, what they do, what are meant to do, you know what I mean? So . . . what they are created for. But ermm I found that there's a lot of difference between them for what you can use. Cos you can use Facebook for more professional things too, and Twitter is like more personal . . . personal.

The idea that social networking tools have set purposes which they are 'created for' influences Paulo's personal use of them and our discussion about them in his assignment. This was explored further in the interview in order for me to get an idea about what he does at home and how this may feed into what goes on at school (or vice versa):

Ibrar: Do you think you have skills from things you do with digital technologies outside of college, which you use to help you inside the college with classwork?
Paulo: Yeah, yeah.
Ibrar: Like what?
Paulo: Like, searching the Internet, searching for new sites, or to make a presentation. Most of the time my mates or my family ask me to help them to use the computer to make Word [files] to make presentations, to make things. My mum, for example, asks me, and I help her. I know new methods to do these.

Here Paulo offers a glimpse into something he does for his mother at home and how he feels he can try or test 'new methods'—most likely learned in college—to aid his family's digital activities. The kind of course that this is, and the nature of this particular assignment, puts Paulo in a good position to be able to evaluate what digital technologies he can use in different situations and for different purposes and to try out the best possible 'new methods' to search sites, make a presentation, etc. A temptation—and mine initially—is to assume that Paulo had answered the reverse of my question: that he has given an example of what he has learned at college which supports his home life. But it is equally likely that as his friends and family come to grips with English-medium digital environments, Paulo's known enthusiasm with ICT activities at college puts him in a situation where he can help people use computers at home and ultimately learn himself as he does so, giving him more confidence in the use of ICTs in the classroom.

When asked more specifically about the assignment, he acknowledges the benefits of using social networks outside of college when it comes to writing about them for assignments, although he doesn't know if those particular technologies will be the subject of an assignment.

Ibrar: Tell me about how you know the social networks that you talked about [in the assignment]?

Paulo: I use them.

Ibrar: For personal or college stuff?

Paulo: Personal. I use it for personal . . . I didn't know if I'm going use it at college or going to talk about it. I think it's easy if you use it before, in your own time; you will know much things about it.

In line with my methodological approach for the interviews, a Venn diagram created during the discussion, and shown in Figure 5.6, helped us to explore further some of the intersections of practices mentioned already and their potential to cross boundaries. The diagram shows that Paulo's Portuguese language blogging remains distinctly a home-based literacy practice, as he chats with friends in Portugal through that medium. Facebook also remains a clearly home-based activity, unlike his use of Myspace:

Ibrar: So Facebook is purely personal?

Paulo: Yeah.

Ibrar: Not at college? Or for college? Remember this part is an overlap [pointing to middle part of Venn diagram]

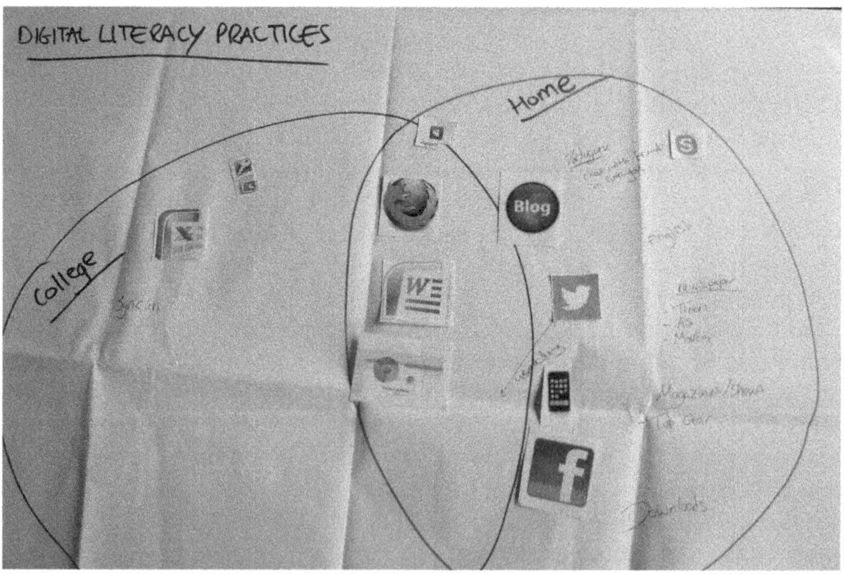

Figure 5.6 Paulo's Venn Diagram

Paulo: Well, my classmates try to add me, but I don't use it for college. But I may use it during college.
Ibrar: But you use Myspace for both?
Paulo: Yeah. Just to talk about college stuff.
Ibrar: College work even?
Paulo: Yeah we can do.

Paulo's friendship networks extend beyond the college, and his social networking activities remain demarcated as such, with classmates trying to add him on Facebook. In a survey carried out across the department by teachers at Northdale College, learners were asked if they would prefer using Facebook for college-related activities (announcements, group communication, etc.). The results were overwhelmingly negative with learners disapproving of its use 'for college' but not—as Paulo states—'during college'. He does not deny the potential for its use to discuss and support college work ("yeah we can do that"), but sticks to the general line that they talk 'about college' on the site. Paulo's keeping this demarcation, and insistence that it is 'just to talk about college' but not 'for college' is consistent with Miller's (2013) 'Global Social Media Impact Study' on 16- to18-year-olds' social networking activities in the UK. In this research, carried out in the same period as the writing of this book,[3] young people have been found to seek out online spaces for social activities separate to those utilised by their parents and in which school activities occur. Facebook use is central to Miller's study and the way that its popularity is apparently being diminished by this shift.

Upon noticing the design of his Venn diagram, I asked Paulo about this demarcation:

Ibrar: Would you say that there's a lot going on in your home, when it comes to digital activities?
Paulo: Yeah.
Ibrar: Which doesn't come to college?
Paulo: No it doesn't.

Here Paulo's response indicates that the demarcation of functions, when it comes to his digital literacy practices, is a deliberate strategy and part of the way he organises his digital life.

Summary

In summary, Paulo had entered a learning environment where he was required to perform a task after being given a set of instructions. This task required his utilisation of a complex set of tools and resources which together, as actors, form an assemblage. Paulo's response to the assignment depended to a certain degree upon how effectively he responded to interactions between these actors: the teacher, the VLE, the ICT support person, etc. Some of these interactions and agencies exert a structuring force on the kinds of literacy practices that Paulo must undertake—or tolerate—during this assignment, and these ultimately lead to choices that have to be made—for example, insistence on VLE utilisation at every stage (from beginning information hunting to final submission). The importance of these literacy practices is actually negligible in that Paulo could hypothetically have completed his assignment without them (i.e. without the VLE). In fact, he may have done it in a shorter time frame without 'enrolment key' problems and other such delays.

Paulo also shows a keenness to organise aspects of the digital literacy practices of his personal and college life in ways that suggest a deliberate separation of these domains, with Facebook used exclusively for outside-college friends and discussions. Wider institutional data reveal that Paulo is not alone in this attitude towards Facebook use; a survey carried out at the college immediately prior to this fieldwork showed that most of the students did not approve of the college's suggested idea of using Facebook for course-related announcements, discussions, etc.

Notes

1 This is at the equivalent level to a UK GCSE, as shown in the QCF (see http://www.accreditedqualifications.org.uk/qualifications-and-credit-framework-qcf.html).

2 Diigo (https://www.diigo.com) is a free social bookmarking and content organising tool.

3 See http://www.ucl.ac.uk/global-social-media for further details of this research.

Part III

6 Buried in the *Matryushkas*

The present is big with the future.

—Leibniz 1714, *Principles of Nature and Grace*[1]

Events and Practices

Theorising in the field of Literacy Studies (e.g. Baynham & Prinsloo, 2009) has problematised the notion of the literacy event and the spatial and temporal characteristics of 'eventness'. Baynham and Prinsloo (2009) in their introduction to *The Future of Literacy Studies* argue that, in relation to literacy events, "once you begin to look more closely there are . . . problems from a number of angles with 'eventness'" (p. 11). One problem with a prototypical notion of an 'event' is an assumption that it can, for the purposes of research and analysis, be neatly differentiated into readily observable and everyday structures, and detached from tangential contexts. To do so risks essentialising or romanticising literacy events, and ignoring broader agencies at play within them.

A detailed and recent work on this particular aspect of literacy has been that of Cathy Kell, whose work in South Africa explores literacy as it is enacted across space and time. Presented as a 'transcontextual' approach, she problematises the notion of locality and localism in literacy research and the limitations of framing one's research as place bounded in ethnographic accounts of literacy. Kell regards this as problematic, since literacy events (as we see with assignments), are not situated neatly in given spaces and times, but are infused with practices which traverse social spaces and time frames. Kell (2006) argues,

> [m]odes and media of communication carry meanings within the streams and flows that make up the texture of the contemporary world, and historically literacy is one of the most important channels through which meanings have crossed space and time.
>
> (Kell, 2006: 147)

Kell's work is of relevance in these case studies of assignment writing. Her work gives further support to the argument that I make in this chapter:

literacy researchers should trace the choreography of practices in a given event, even if it takes one beyond their site of interest. Operationalising Latour's (2005) injunction to 'follow the actors' and to 'trace associations', Law (2012) instructs social researchers to "[f]irst attend to practices . . . look to see what is being done" (Law, 2012: 171).[2] From an account of the practices, we can get an idea of the world that is emerging through them and how that world is "assembled and ordered to produce objects, subjects and appropriate locations". Through this framing, we get to see how events such as assignments are emergent in practices and how some of these practices jostle with one another in the choices and dilemmas faced by students when using digital media in the classroom.

Through an examination of the various levels of practice involved to inform, assemble, and ultimately write an assignment, we can see that the number of actors engaged in the writing process can become far-reaching, even if they are disparate conceptually. Law further writes, "once we turn up the magnification we quickly find that there isn't an independent, prior, definite, singular and coherent real out there upon which the various reports of reality are based" (Law, 2012: 171). This perspective to sociology highlights an interconnectedness of all matter which, as I have argued in Chapter 2, draws from Deleuze's work on the philosopher and mathematician Gottfried Wilhelm Leibniz:

> Every portion of matter can be thought of as a garden full of plants, or as a pond full of fish. But every branch of the plant, every part of the animal, and every drop of its vital fluids, is another such garden, or another such pond.
>
> (von Leibniz *et al.*, 1998: 277)

If we increase the magnification upon the practices of assignment writing in this study, other literacy events lie within them. In this way, some of the things that became evident in the previous chapters were how Sara, Anne, and Paulo accomplished the following:

1. They mobilised and drew upon texts external to the immediate situation (e.g. online reports, other assignments, assessment criteria). These were written in different locations, by different people, at different times, and with different purposes, but influentially shaped the task at hand.
2. They engaged in digital literacy practices which were unsanctioned, and in some cases prohibited, by the normative digital culture of the college. These practices often aided content creation and are discussed in in Chapter 8 as moments of *irruption*.
3. They pointed to the salience of future literacy events. This included intending to use their present work as validation for future assignments by saving their work in archive folders within a complex digital filing system on personal pen drives.

4 They managed the sometimes obscure procedure that lay behind the tasks, such as specific protocols to access assignment instructions and to submit their work for marking. These originated from other actors (e.g. managerial directives and 'good practice' guides) with their origins and locations far beyond the event being observed.

The aforementioned instances from the three cases show that we cannot understand the literacy practices of the classroom exclusively through what occurs inside its four walls. Much is conflated, with many actors not immediately present, yet vital to any critical understanding of digital literacy. For example, as Paulo wrote his assignment, perhaps his teacher was concerned with her next appraisal, as she sought to adhere rigidly to the college's digital learning standards document throughout the lesson. These standards, set by the teacher in the classroom, resulted in 'hoops' for students such as Paulo to 'jump through'. And she, in turn, had her own hoops to jump through. In this way, practices are never coherent, nor are they predictable; therefore, they do not perform a truly coherent reality, as Law makes clear:

> Coherence is simply an aspiration. In practice, practices are always more or less non-coherent. They work by enacting different versions of reality and more or less successfully holding these together . . . If we look for non-coherences within practices we will find them. We will discover collateral realities.
>
> (Law, 2012: 175)

Actors that are behind the scenes in this complex assemblage can also be said to include educational managers of the college, the education system, the state, and so on. What emerges as we examine the practices and follow the actors are tasks nested within tasks, literacy practices within events, and further practices and events indicated by those—such as matryushka dolls. For example, when Paulo is instructed to retrieve information from the VLE, there are a number of things he must do: i) open a browser and find the VLE online, ii) log in with his username and password, iii) navigate the menu system, etc. Each of these is a story of practices that is not straightforward and sometimes fraught with choices and dilemmas, such as his failing to log in and his needing to call an ICT support person to re-enter the room to work around the problem.

It therefore becomes Sara's, Anne's, and Paulo's, and the multitude of other actors', *contextualising practices* which become more important rather than simply the *context* of the scenario I have entered (c.f. Edwards, 2009). In this vein, and by following the actors, and tracing their associations, we can get to the practices that Law speaks about. And here we find, echoing Leibniz's conception, practices within events, which indicate further events with more practices—unconfined to any particular and a priori representation of place (e.g. 'classroom') or time (e.g. 'lesson').

A related notion within the interdisciplinary field of Literacy Studies has been suggested already by Brandt and Clinton (2002) who call us to question the "limits of the local" in literacy research and for it to take into account the "larger enterprises . . . away from the immediate scene" (Brandt and Clinton, 2002: 338) in the situational here and now of events. This leads us to question *where* and *when* literacy events are identified. While the cases outlined in this research are chronicled at specific times and places, the literacy practices themselves spill over into different temporal and spatial realms, and can circulate in cross-network practices of re-contextualisation—for example, Anne writing through her assessment criteria and Sara's re-working some text from her previous assignment.

In many ways, the assignments can themselves be seen as 'collateral realities' (c.f. Law) in the life histories of the students. They are incidental products, perhaps to be forgotten in later years, but nevertheless necessary both to get through the lesson, the module aims, and, more broadly, for the students' future lives and careers. As an event, it thereby becomes encased by other dolls with time.

Assembling the Assignment

Moving on from the discussion in the previous section, we can describe assignments as being 'assembled' by the practices at play in a literacy event. An assignment's apparent end completion therefore suggests a reality that is really an *effect* of the bundles of practices choreographed to attain that effect. This is the "performativity of practice" (Law, 2012: 161), and it necessitates that careful attention be paid to the ecology of student practices in a literacy event to see how sociomaterial relations are assembled and their realities (such as assignments) are done. In other words, the cultural order of the literacy event is held together by an assemblage of competing and disparate practices, some of which are elided from view, pushed out of the way, or unacknowledged. This *performative* conceptualisation of digital literacies holds that digital literacy practices, and all the actors that they bring with them (texts, friends, algorithms, etc.), perform the reality of the assignment. This also holds true for other entities such as the classroom, the timetable, the game play, etc., which are deemed as residual effects of practices and relations. Effects such as these are not to be assumed as a priori facts in an ANT account; rather, we must trace the practices and associations that assemble them to appear this way.

From this orientation, therefore, an investigation of a student sitting at his or her classroom desk writing an assignment begins with the view that entities such as the teacher, the student, the class, the assignment, etc., are all performed through an assemblage of practices which make them who or what they are. It thus begs to be asked of the product that emerges from those practices: 'how does it come to be as it is?' and 'could it be done differently?'

Thus, in the examination of written assignment work for this study, what eventually came to be known and recognised by all those involved as an 'assignment' was assembled through a choreography of practices and performances of these practices. By looking not only at the outcome of an assignment (that it was done well and on time) but also at the practices that held it together, this research identified the layered and nested practices of students and the often 'messy' and contested ways they interact on intersecting spatial and temporal planes. These practices, as the three cases reveal, originated from different domains (friendship groups, family chats, work-based reports, etc.), yet they were mobilised into the assignment-writing event in the classroom and collectively assembled as the precarious entity of the assignment. Examples include the use of personal chats and social arrangements (Sara), presentation files done at home with family and first-language blogging (Paulo), and the embedding of Twitter and Pinterest (Anne). Overlapping through these practices are *other* assemblage identities (the Facebook friend, the helpful bilingual son, the teaching professional, etc.) which are themselves fashioned and managed through these very practices, all intersecting within a shared space and time. What, therefore, remains exclusively 'academic' or 'vernacular' in the digital literacy practices for an assignment is moot, and to label practices this way would get in the way of how I am trying to theorise them.

Instead, digital literacy emerges as a bundled and performative act, as opposed to monolithic and predictive. By investigating these nested and complex practices using scrutinising methodologies, such as the multimethod and videographic techniques adopted in this study,[3] an assignment materialised as much more than the file on a student's computer. In Chapter 7 and Chapter 8, I examine some of these more nested digital literacy practices through presenting and discussing the notions of 'curation' and 'irruption'.

If the sociomaterial work done to complete the assignments is successful, a number of hegemonic forces, hurdles, and resistances need to be overcome, and it is within these resistances, or moments of 'jostling', that interesting digital literacy practices lie. For Sara, Anne, and Paulo, successful assignment completion relied upon these "sub rosa" (cf. Gilmore, 1986) or 'secret' digital literacy practices. The role these sub rosa digital literacies can play in the completion of assignments can be profound, yet when students are judged against them, they are deemed either as rule breakers or not competent in the dominant literacy. The assignments appear to be created and maintained by this network of practices and actors which themselves are aligned for the purposes of an assignment (i.e. in practice) but separate and disparate otherwise.

Precariousness

Practices appear to hold the assignment together, but a close examination of them shows that they do so only through precarious interactions with each other. These practices work to maintain the durability of a prototypical reality of the assignment by engaging and drawing on a network of actors such as policies and policymakers, college management, digital learning frameworks, etc. But this reality is far from uncontested. This is because as Sara, Anne, and Paulo engaged with the assignments, they were not only creating *new networks* of their own, but they were also leveraging literacies that otherwise have no place in the classroom to help them get their work done, including digital literacy practices enacted by more local and global assemblages that were institutional, vocational, personal, etc., in character.

For example, in a very brief moment during Sara's assignment writing, she discusses the contents of her assignment with the teacher, her friend sitting next to her, and another friend on Facebook via her own device (which, by the way, contravenes college policies on classroom ICT use). Whilst doing this, she also scrolls through reports from her previous employer's website, and, among other things, dips into a previous assignment on a related topic. The relations between these actors is not stable in this brief moment of digital literacy; they rely on various actors working together collectively to hold the very moment together. These are far-reaching actors such as personal devices (used beneath the table to avoid being noticed), friends who are online and available, chat applications, Internet connections effectively working, etc. All of these far-reaching actors now become part of the assemblage. The composite result of all of the relational practices between the actors is content for Sara's assignment in that particular moment. To understand assignment writing, therefore, an empirical examination of the practices that the students engaged in to produce them is necessary. Also important are the ways in which those practices were organised and systematised as part of their writing strategies, and how they gained their meaning and function as dynamic elements of something else and from somewhere else entirely.

The kinds of writing and literacies which are meant to emerge in the assignments are those which are commensurate with a particular and college-centric notion of 'digital literacy'. This notion is held up by certain structuring agencies and their actors already discussed: the colleges' acceptable use policies, good practice guides, and general classroom procedures. All of these lead to a top-down imposed notion of what digital literacy is and how it should be applied. This, in turn, regulates the teachers' actions and decisions which subsequently end up mostly to do with channelling students' access to particular digital media and in particular ways as they orchestrate a replication of managerial and policy diktat. This runs contrary to the learners' bricolage of practices. We can draw upon an intellectual antecedent to the ANT tradition to further illuminate the precariousness of practices: Deleuze and Guattari's (1987; 2004) distinction between the rhizome and tree structures.

The metaphorical difference between a tree structure and a rhizome structure is that a tree structure is hierarchical with knowledge organised systematically from stems to roots. The rhizome, however, overturns the standardised approach of the tree structure with its multidimensionality, fluidity, and branching out into places unexpected. The rhizome is therefore the antithesis of the tree and is characterised by its heterogeneity, multiplicity, flow, and fluidity:

> Unlike trees or their roots, the rhizome connects any point to any other point, and its traits are not necessarily linked to traits of the same nature . . . The rhizome is reducible to neither the One nor the multiple . . . It is composed not of units but of dimensions, or rather directions in motion. It has neither beginning nor end, but always in a middle (*milieu*) from which it grows and which it overspills . . . [it] operates by variation, expansion, conquest, capture, offshoot . . . it has multiple entryways and its own lines of flight.
>
> (Deleuze & Guattari, 2004: 23)

In this respect, Deleuze and Guattari's rhizome metaphor connects with tenets of ANT, its intellectual successor project, by conceptualising rhizomes as entanglements of humans and non-humans. This is through their alliances or 'assemblages' (a word shared by both traditions). The dictum, therefore, is to follow the actors and their associations. Moreover, according to Michael Lynch (in Latour, 1999), ANT should actually be named "actant-rhizome ontology", with the blatant reference to Deleuze and Guattari in that particular coinage. ANT as a theoretical tradition, however, also draws from ethnomethodology and later became popular as a more developed method for analysing scientific and technological knowledge-building practices.

The concurrent work possible through digital media, the co-presence of practices, and the ubiquitous nature of digital media, along with a continuous supply of Wi-Fi/cellular coverage, allow for the widespread possibility of rhizomatic literacy practices. Parsons and Clarke (2013) make a case that the Internet engenders "rhizomatic thinking" and that prolific web users are like rhizomes themselves. Drawing on Deleuze and Guattari (1987; 2004), they contend,

> If young people can be thought of as rhizomes, any point of a rhizome can connect to any other point. Youth have few firewalls. They celebrate privacy, and simultaneously welcome infringement. They build barriers (think of iPods) to eliminate barriers (think of listening to music from anywhere), becoming more rhizomatic as they do; their presence is like an invasion to a newly envisioned world.
>
> (Parsons & Clarke, 2013: 90)

To think rhizomatically about Sara, Anne, and Paulo's digital literacy practices is to focus on the choreography of relations between entities that may otherwise be thought of as discrete: friendship groups, algorithms, writers of government reports, computer programmers in Silicon Valley, families, the local primary school, etc. Their sub rosa digital literacy practices, and other such enactments, are characteristic examples of rhizomatic thinking and assignment-writing strategies. Their teachers, however, tried to regulate them into following a top-down approach.

This draws us to the debates surrounding how writing as an activity is conceptualised in digital environments. The ideas discussed in this chapter, drawing on ANT and assemblage theory, support wider inquiries into how the Internet is used in student writing and the nature of originality and plagiarism. Work which problematises students' Internet-supported writing strategies—for example, studies of "patchwriting" (Pecorari, 2003)—has drawn attention to the importance of better understanding how students appropriate web resources as they write for assignments. Patchwriting is a way to describe the rearrangement of texts with little of a new author's actual voice in the final written product. Another related concept is that of "pseudo-writing" (Skaar, 2014), which refers to student writing that is aided by web-based resources to such an extent that ideas are not translated by the writer, but merely transposed to another context. Appropriating web-based sources, therefore, reduces the cognitive work carried out as part of the writing process. The argument in both cases is that the plethora of content on the Internet can promote assignment-writing strategies which call into question a classical notion of originality in assignment writing.

At its core, however, these debates centre on the primordial question of what it means to be literate. A topic on which debate endures from a time when Socrates voiced concerns that literacy (*sensu* writing) had deleterious effects on memory and from which numerous fields of research have produced volumes of work. Once again, this argument needs revision to acknowledge the new digital environments within which literacies have become contested. By looking not only at the outcome of a literacy activity (e.g. an assignment), but at the practices that constitute it and give it its character, we get a more accurate picture of the many agencies at play in modern digital literacy. If we open up the matryushkas, we get a more detailed picture of how students respond to educational tasks. With the practices laid out and unbundled before us, we can then accurately see what is happening in literacy events and make sufficient claims about digital literacies. But to do this necessitates two things. First, we need a methodological shift to 'follow actors' and go beyond the particular site being observed to better understand the convoluted digital literacies emerging in classroom activities. And second, we need to cast a critical lens upon the previously unproblematised actors (e.g. software developers, algorithms) which have come to shape the new kinds of literacy practices occurring in classrooms.

Notes

1 In Latta (1898: 373).
2 See Chapter 2 for a fuller discussion.
3 See Bhatt *et al.* (2015) and Bhatt (2017) for a full discussion.

7 Curation as Digital Literacy Practice

> The writer can only imitate a gesture that is always anterior, never original. His only power is to mix writings, to counter the ones with the others, in such a way as never to rest on any one of them.
>
> —(Barthes & Heath, 1977: 146)

Information-Thick Worlds

In the classrooms I observed, teaching practices were altered by compliance with digital learning strategies and managerial policies. These ultimately had a significant and far-reaching impact on the practices of assignment writing. The interplay of the diverse array of digital literacy practices, and the multiple and sometimes conflicting actors involved, rendered much of what happened during the writing of the assignments as in flux and not always predictable. The previous chapter on the nested nature of digital literacies demonstrates how the multiple and sometimes conflicting actors, induced by new technologies and policies, play out within the classroom and through writing itself. By looking further at students' methodologies and strategies in doing their assignments, we can clearly see an emergence and interplay of individualistic practices which navigate the course of writing. Prominent among these practices are what I describe in this chapter as *curation*. This is a dynamic term which is described in more detail later in the chapter, but is characterised by the students' judicious and purposeful assimilation, aggregation, and harnessing of digital content in order to produce something new.

Fitting with the information theorist Edward Tufte's (1990) conception that follows, other related theories (e.g. Antonio *et al.*, 2012; White, 2012; Snyder, 2015), and traditional and contemporary connotations of the word, this chapter argues that many of the practices employed by Sara, Anne, and Paulo were sophisticated and yet self-taught acts of digital curation. The purpose of this chapter, therefore, is not just to try to develop a theory of curation as a digital literacy practice but also to reflect upon how we perceive educational end products such as assignments with curation as a central component.

According to Tufte (1990), people are able to thrive in what he describes as "information thick worlds" (p. 50) primarily through a range of everyday practices, including the ability to

> select, edit, single out, structure, highlight, group, pair, merge, harmonize, synthesize, focus, organize, condense, reduce, boil down, choose, categorize, catalog, classify, list, abstract, scan, look into, idealize, isolate, discriminate, distinguish, screen, pigeonhole, pick over, sort, integrate, blend, inspect, filter, lump, skip, smooth, chunk, average, approximate, cluster, aggregate, outline, summarize, itemize, review, dip into, flip through, browse, glance into, leaf through, skim, refine, enumerate, glean, synopsize, winnow the wheat from the chaff, and separate the sheep from the goats.
>
> (Tufte, 1990: 50)

The processes of searching and harnessing old content to produce new content is elaborately outlined by Tufte and broadly follows my notion of curation. The word curation derives from the Latin root *curare*, which means 'to cure' or 'to take care of'. Historically, curation relates to processes of organisation, collation, judicious selection for presentation purposes, and even curing and preserving. The term has conventionally been applied to such work carried out in museum settings and has now evolved to describe what is often done in digital environments and in online social, personal, educational, and commercial spaces (Rosenbaum, 2011). Consistent with the notion of curation in art and museum contexts, recent conceptualisations of 'digital content curation' are based on the collation and organisation of content around a theme for a particular special interest or purpose. How information is discovered and managed plays a pivotal role in the current digital media landscape and then becomes a specialist type of creative labour in and of itself.

Ilana Snyder (2015), who takes a social practice look at curation, sees it as a subjective and ideological process in which curators select existing objects to construct their own 'truths' (Snyder, 2015: 211). Through this production, it becomes a type of "individual creative practice and self-presentation" (Snyder, 2015). In the view of Rosenbaum, who distinguishes between content creation, content curation, and content aggregation, Snyder's description would incorporate both content creation and content curation. Rosenbaum thereby breaks down an overarching concept of *content management* into the following categories (in Snyder, 2015: 212–214):

1. *Content creation* involves the development of newsworthy, educational, and entertainment material for distribution over the Internet or other electronic media.
2. *Content aggregation* involves the automatic gathering of links achieved through the computerised processes of "gathering, organising and

filtering content" (Snyder, 2015: 213). Content aggregation exists largely as algorithmically managed (big) data and is distinguishable by its *seeming* objectivity and its exogenous nature. Aggregation is primarily about profit making and the algorithms ostensibly place no value on truth, accuracy, or morality. That determination lies in the hands of a human curator.

3 *Content curation*, or editorial curation, involves human filtering and organising, and is an expanding practice online in which people (note the human element) add their work to that of the machines. What makes content curation different from the systematic aggregation and syndication of content is that it is editorially selected and enhanced, as well as a form of added value (Snyder, 2015: 214).

Content creation and content aggregation have been used primarily for online marketing, analysing the interests of web users, and presenting them with a bespoke information environment (ads, goods, etc.). It is a computerised attempt at representing the mind of the consumer. The implications of this algorithmic work and their representations must be considered, and they will be discussed later in this chapter.

Content creation is arguably the most demanding requirement of curation and the factor that is most influential in making curation transformative. By adding meaning or expanding a narrative on a subject, we extend the relevance of that idea, that act of creativity, or that literacy event into the future with the possibility of it being carried into perpetuity. This kind of creativity—or re-combining pre-existing content to fabricate new content—has been dubbed by some as 'remix' (Lessig, 2008; Gunkel, 2016) and described as a practice that is "the very nature of the digital" (Gibson, 2005). Knobel and Lankshear's (2008) argument for 'creative remix' looks similar. They say that "classroom pedagogy stands to learn much from remix (content creation) practices and smart tools and how they enable learning and achievement" (p. 30).

The digital world presents us with complex new assemblages, corresponding and adaptive practices, and a mind-boggling amount of content. Filtering that content is a literacy practice, and filtering it prudently for purposes of academic work is a skill set. Howard Rheingold (2012) has written extensively about the kinds of skills which can support effective digital content curation. He refers to a sort of critical mindfulness amid the massive sea of information available to anyone who searches the web. He refers to this as 'crap detection' and argues that if students fail to assess the credibility of Internet sources effectively, then the web's usefulness as a reliable source of information is in jeopardy. Crap detection, Rheingold (2012) argues, is essential to manage and effectively negotiate through the mass of information present in today's digital environments and, subsequently, for curation purposes.

The way that students manage that negotiation and their subsequent curation practices during assignment writing is therefore critical. Through examining the digital literacies of assignment writing, we can see evidence of curation, often as part of intrinsic writing strategies. Specifically, and as a basis for the discussion that follows, content curation shall be identified as a process consisting of (1) *problematising an issue or topic,* (2) *anthologising and aggregating information relevant to a topic and enlisting filters to manage it,* (3) *applying impressionistic and editorial discretion to appeal to and reach a target audience,* (4) *adding value to pre-existing content by contributing new or extended meaning and/or creating a new narrative,* and (5) *presenting that data in the appropriately determined platform.*

With regard to this conception of curation, there are two main areas of discussion emerging from this research. First, in completing their assignments, each student in the account that follows demonstrated such acts of curation. Second, an assignment itself may or may not explicitly require students to engage in these practices, and this tells us something about how assignment tasks, as tools for assessment, can be conceptualised and designed.

Curating Assignments

Sara

In Sara's assignment, initial curation took the form of gathering and assembling material from her well-archived folders of previously completed work, adding new information as specifically outlined in her task instructions, and finally methodically storing her work for submission and reuse. Sara began working on her assignment immediately after the class reconvened following the break and, being task oriented, she made clearly deliberate decisions about how she would begin. Indeed, part of curation as I present it here is about conceptualising a target audience and reconstituting information to meet its needs. Sara continuously asking the teacher and other students what she should be doing in order to make sure that her assignment would meet the requirements of the intended audience was, thus, part of the curation of her assignment. Added to this, much of Sara's initial editorial decision making began from her previous assignment. She knew that the teacher, whom she recognised as the immediate intended audience, approved of a certain font, style, and structure. Therefore, Sara copied those elements directly from her previous work. These are curation practices which rely on the validity and established nature of previous strategies. They are a safe template to work from. In Sara's assignment case, we must look at how and why this is the case and what holds this set of practices together, and more importantly, how and why would they get disregarded.

Throughout the class period, Sara recalled her previous work to guide her assignment writing. She did this meticulously and methodically, and there are two main things at play here. First, she had devised this as her overall strategy. Since each assignment is like a new reality, she needed some referential reality in which to place it. She began by looking through old assignments to see how she might have addressed the same topic in the past, extracted that content, and inserted it into an assignment 'shell' she had prefabricated from another old assignment. This gave her a template, a reference point, and some written material to work from. She and her friend Lauren saw this as a sort of shortcut to completing the assignment. Also contained within this work involving the previous assignment are editorial practices, as mentioned earlier, regarding the preferences of her audience.

Sara faced a couple of problems doing this, including finding a proper fit to the current assignment. By employing curation strategies which draw in erstwhile assignments, she ran into difficulty. Fifteen minutes into the session, Sara was still considering how to integrate the contents of previous assignment/s into the current one. She eventually negotiated the requirements of the new assignment with both old and new content, but it is unknown if she lost some opportunity to add more value or contribution to the discussion by reintroducing the old. Also, she did this in spite of the teacher's urging that she and Lauren should not merely copy and paste from other work.

While Sara showed adeptness in determining her objective and committing herself to complete the task, the difficulties she faced are also noteworthy. As resources, the past assignments make for safe options to reference and incorporate into this task, especially over free and open web searching, which, as Sara found, can lead to nowhere. In fact, she spent a great deal of time hunting for information online, and in each instance, there were suggestions thrown up at her in the search results. This was the intervention of the algorithm working out what it 'thought' she wanted or should be viewing. In one of such moments, Sara's confusion lay in the search for a "child protection act 1999" which she had been directed to via Google, only to be told by her teacher that Google's suggestion was incorrect, as it showed legislation from another country and subsequently was not relevant to her assignment. This points to weaknesses in her search strategy as she must not have considered the expansive nature of the results. For Sara, editing and crap detection in this assignment began with how she searched for information and discerned misinformation.

Looking at the data of Sara's assignment recording sequentially shines further light on the amount of time Sara spent following misinformation, talking about what to do, and not finding any substantially useful content for the assignment. It was only after an hour that she decided to go back again to the previous assignments (having begun in this way) and attempt to garner information to copy, paste, and rehash into the current assignment since the contents overlapped.

Sara's competency in acts of digital content curation are therefore mixed. Conducting an inefficient search and then being misled by the Google algorithm demonstrates an inability to effectively filter or discern appropriateness of content. Reliance on cutting and pasting from old assignments and online sources might not be the best strategy, or produce the most novel or insightful work, but it is sufficient and an astute way to complete this assignment. Where Sara excels, however, is in developing clever workaround techniques to circumvent any ineffectuality in content curation. Where content creation is not required or not highly valued, this digital literacy practice may be the most useful of all.

The difficulties Sara faced point to strategies to improve not just her own acuity in content curation but also how her assignment could be designed with these practices in mind. We will return to this aspect at the end of this chapter, alongside similar insights from the other two cases. While Sara did not add much value to the narrative on policies concerning the safeguarding of children (the topic of her assignment), she nonetheless managed to complete her assignment on time and also saved her work as a template in preparation for the next iteration of curation required for a future assignment. In this way, her curation strategies are deliberately cyclical.

Anne

It should first be noted that Anne's class is composed of teachers undergoing professional development courses, and this makes them older than most other students at the college. This has created a distinct work environment and learning space which is more conducive to curation. For example, I saw that the students in Anne's class were given more freedom to work on their assignment as compared to the other two case studies. The following quote from a blog post written by Anne's tutor shows that with this increased freedom, the students were expected to create content for assessment using their own judgement and filters:

> I cannot dictate the contents of the assignment to the learners and how they should present their work. This is kind of the point of this course. They are required to selectively research and evaluate technologies in their own practice.[1]

Consequently, Anne's discriminative use of filters and demarcations was employed throughout the writing of her portfolio. Her distinct roles as student, teacher, and educational professional became evident immediately when the session began, and when Anne began writing in her personal reflective blog as opposed to her course group blog. The recording showed her tweaking a previously written text to be included on her blog and linking it to her digital portfolio. Consciously differentiating between the two blogs shows an acknowledgement of her audience, her message, and her digital platform. Tailoring the content to her audience by softening its perceived critical force is also indicative of judicious curation, particularly in terms of the kinds of meaning-making that only a human's curation can achieve.

Anne's assignment was to create a digital portfolio of her reflections on the use of technology in the learning environment, and it was one that required curation by its design. As a required component of the assignment, Anne was required to 'signpost' within the portfolio, rendering much of her text as hyperlinked to other places including articles, blog posts, and personal reflections which draw from her roles as student and teacher. The nature of the assignment itself requires content aggregation, reflection, creation, and the discernment of the roles of self and audience for appropriate content. It was an assignment of curation, and yet it differed significantly from Paulo's in ways that will be discussed later when I turn to strategies for teaching curation practices. The main difference mentioned here is that instead of having a clear deterministic end point, Anne's assignment was open-ended and encouraged uniqueness arising from the subjective experience of each student, as their experience informed each of their blogs, which ultimately informed their digital portfolio.

Anne, who maintained both personal and professional blogs at the time of writing the assignment, was meticulous in the way she discriminated between the purpose, intent, and audience of each blog and how she signposted from them and other online sources into her digital portfolio. Her discriminating ability helped her manage the boundary crossings that occurred from having multiple identities in her online life. Maintaining her digital portfolio required her to confront those overlapping assemblage identities: Anne as student, teacher, and critical educational professional. For example, she embedded her tweets in her blog, most of which were about what is happening in the educational sector in which she works. She then linked her blog to her digital portfolio, in which she wrote in the capacity of a student. She also bookmarked links, mostly related to her role as teacher, in Diigo and then embedded the Diigo file in her digital portfolio. The assignment brief required that she not only identify her audience but also her point of view. By maintaining clearly defined roles and parameters, instantiated in her Venn diagram as part of our interview (see Chapter 3), she managed this complex role judiciously.

We also saw Anne encounter a snag in doing her assignment while copying and pasting between multiple tabs online. This existed as a technical glitch with Moodle, which retained some embedded information from the site of the copied text into the site she pasted into. Throughout her assignment, Anne pasted links from Twitter, her blogs, and other places online with proficiency, and even when a technical glitch arose from Moodle, she had the skills to solve it. She clearly developed creative and improvisatory workaround abilities to address what she described as 'the foibles of jumping' between platforms (see Chapter 3). Because of the ease and proficiency with which she conducted complex acts of curation, and also because of the design of the assignment as an explicitly curated one, Anne's case is quite informative for what it can tell us about the relationship between acts of curation and digital literacy.

Her selection of what to include—and what not to—therefore becomes important, as she seemed readily able to mobilise and utilise resources from various domains (work, study, and home) and integrate them into her digital portfolio. The digital portfolio itself, in turn, influences Anne's practices with digital literacy in her outside-college life by being one of the many institutional actors pushing the icons of her Venn diagram (see Chapter 3) into the middle to create a crossover with her home and student practices. Also, the fact that the nature of the course and the demographics of the class were more conducive to curation could be an obvious reason why Anne was more successful in composing a well-curated assignment. And in that there are also lessons to be learned.

Paulo

Paulo's case study is illuminating for what it can inform us about assignment design and how an assignment can encourage (or discourage) content curation. His assignment was presented to the students in his class via multiple platforms: an instructional handout, via the Moodle VLE, the whiteboard display, and verbally outlined by the teacher. Each of these came with numerous guidelines and very specific instructions, and each version was worded slightly differently. This caused confusion for Paulo and others in the classroom. After initial uncertainty, the recording shows Paulo thinking momentarily before getting to work. We might assume he had reflected upon the multiple versions of the assignment instructions, aggregated that information into one task, and strategised what needed to be done. He initiated his work by logging on to the VLE as instructed, but was denied access. Following ten minutes of frustration and disengagement because of technical problems, Paulo finally moved forwards by abandoning the VLE and opening his writing assignment in Word.

He got into the flow of writing, going back and forth between Word, different web pages, his assignment instructions, and, ultimately, Google searches. It was largely after the class technology component broke down that Paulo, who was inherently interested and personally familiar with the topic of his assignment, gathered his thoughts and his prepared notes to begin writing. As he wrote, there were constant reminders from the teacher about the structure and purpose that the assignment's content must adhere to. While Paulo continued typing through the teacher's background instructions, he was acutely mindful of the intent, audience, and criteria his assignment needed to address. These being the principles of good curation, he collated from past assignments, online sources, data he had gathered, and personal experience to curate for his assignment.

We can view Paulo's assignment as having been designed, in part, to teach a methodology of curation. In demonstrating an ability to perform certain tasks in certain ways (to 'jump through hoops', see Chapter 4 and Chapter 6), the students would be judged to have performed curation to complete their assignment. But they were simply being required to complete an assignment of curation without seriously needing to assess the issue at hand and content, nor apply editorial discretion, or use their abilities to aggregate information. Partially to aid the second-language student writers of the class with their composition, it was predetermined what each paragraph should address, what type of words should be used, and from where their data and contents should come. However, that Paulo nonetheless used varied outside sources, used his own experience with technology to add value to the discussion, and blogged about this assignment to a different audience, shows some of the ingenuity and improvisation of his curation—albeit at times not in conformance to the methodology prescribed by the teacher.

The course, having an ICT inflection, influenced how the teacher designed the assignment and conducted the classes. She made an emphatic point of having the students access course and assignment-related material via the VLE, and she even outlined this as part of the process of actually 'doing' the assignment. She also repeatedly pushed the students to curate their assignment using the Diigo roll she had aggregated, which contained selected links related to the assignment.

The teacher's insistence on using the VLE evolves from requirements within the college's digital learning standards document. This document divides the quality of digital media deployment for learning and teaching into three standards (bronze, silver, and gold), and it is used as a basis for judging the quality of its use in lessons during inspections and quality assurance processes. It is clear from her steadfast insistence on accomplishing tasks in strategic ways that she was guided by the standards and their evaluation. According to the criteria as set out in the standards document, to achieve a mere 'bronze' level of ICT use, a teacher must ensure that

- students actively use the VLE for resources and information
- students access the resources from the VLE during each lesson
- assignment work support is available online from the VLE

Where she could have simply handed out the assignment details and allowed the students to curate their assignment individually and freely, she instead invokes specific material actors in establishing a set of procedures to get things done. For example, by placing the instructions on the VLE for Paulo to access along with a list of links in the Diigo roll, she established a set of procedural hoops for him to jump through as part of the task. That procedural rubric directed her instructional practices over the span of the assignment event and manifested itself in several ways. Also, the way she implemented a series of procedural instructions shows that she is under her own instructions to use technologies a certain way in her teaching and has to get students to obtain information in a certain way. She therefore has her *own* hoops to jump through.

The way this is most strongly borne out is in the creation of the assignment itself. Like the aggregative digital portfolio assignment in Anne's case, Paulo's assignment has a pervasive element of *pre-curation* within it. The assignments are pre-curated in that here aggregation and evaluation are not inherent requirements with delineations. And it is not until the students add their own impressionistic evaluation, and discernment, that the assignment outcome is considered curated as defined in this chapter. What must be addressed, then, are the actors which pre-curate.

The policies are actors which direct and dictate how the teacher employs ICT in the classroom to attain at least a bronze level designation. But as actors, they also attempt to determine a particular type of assignment end product for Paulo. According to these guiding actors, the assignment should be one whose content is drawn from pre-selected and curated resources placed in the VLE and organised using Diigo to attain a certain level of equivalence across all the students' work. Furthermore, in accordance with the teacher's instructions, it should have a specified layout, address specific issues in certain ways whilst using specific types of words, and use specified technologies to accomplish set objectives. An insidious side effect is seen in the teacher's resultant preference for standardised and equivalent student submissions. By insisting on using Diigo's list of supported links, the importance of independently searching the web and utilising discretion and discernment to determine appropriateness for the task is minimised. Just as Paulo was beginning to achieve a creative flow to his work, on numerous occasions he was interrupted by the teacher to bring him back on track to the procedure-compliant, standards-based, normative, and pre-curated assignment. Clearly, this stands in opposition to a good practice of digital curation—one in which Paulo has to discern the quality of his information himself and deeply consider his audience.

An assignment such as this which is closed from both its front-ends (through prescribed methods of gathering content) and back-ends (through submission protocols) cannot really promote a free and open kind of curation. It is encouraging to see that despite this, and when the technology also failed, Paulo had the skills to overcome and resort to his own acts of curation. This was exemplified well after repeated insistence from the teacher to use the Diigo roll to access her aggregated list of supported resources. Paulo did so, but the Diigo link did not work. Because Paulo had already been hunting for information through Google and Google.pt (Portuguese) on his own, he was not set back. He used his own discretion and experience to guide him.

During this entire period, Paulo went about his assignment in a way that he saw most appropriate for himself, even using his first language to aid him during Google searching. In doing this and in the way he searched for a video to aid him in creating a requisite graph, Paulo showed an ability to aggregate information, an understanding of what information he sought to corroborate his point in the report being written, and a knowledge of how and where to attain that information. Finally, it is worth noting that Paulo blogged about his assignment once he had completed it, thereby addressing another, different, audience.

One of the objectives of the digital learning standards at Northdale College is to use technologies "to improve student opportunities for learning". The document also states that the evidence required to attain a 'gold standard' of achievement is demonstrated by such things as the design of courses which insist on access to information and resources through the VLE. It is therefore important to consider who or what these policies are actually addressing and the kinds of digital literacy—and learning—practices that play out when they are applied so emphatically by teachers such as Paulo's.

Curation, Digital Literacies, and Assignments

Earlier in Chapter 2, I discussed the benefit of viewing the assignment as a literacy event. This aspect of the event has been explored in Chapter 6. When looked at in this way, what we find in each of the cases studied is that the curation of information necessary for the completion of the assignments sometimes ran into snags, and the students had varied and individual practices to address them. Looking at these snags, they present themselves in a number of ways including working old assignments into new work, handling misinformation, the foibles of moving between platforms, and jumping through procedural hoops. While they are certainly revealing insofar as what they tell us about the digital literacies of students, they are perhaps more revealing in what we can deduce about learning, and what we can conclude about teaching.

To better elucidate those conclusions, we find this strategy of looking at the literacy event through the lens of curation particularly useful in that it brings to attention the evolving role of students as authors, 'remixers', and curators, and the literacy practices that position them this way. And this, in turn, makes easier the pedagogic challenge of finding a way to acknowledge and then harness these literacy practices, against current normative models of digital literacy and traditional conceptions of authorship, upon which students' writing is often assessed.

What we have seen is that each student applied a type of digital literacy to the doing of the assignment that was not taught as part of the assignment. Skills which they may have nurtured within the home, work, or institutional 'underlife' (Goffman, 1961) were applied when they encountered snags. That Sara said laughingly of the VLE Moodle, "you don't need to know it, people only use what they need to use," and Paulo said, "I didn't learn new work . . . but I think I did [the assignment] well," indicate the degree to which these digital research skills are already inculcated into their repertoire of practices. And, indeed, the transferability of these digital literacies across multiple domains and types of content is what makes them so transformative to the students' academic experience and ultimately what made them successful in their assignments.

What should one make of the determination that Paulo could have completed his assignment without being present in the class? What about that while Sara did not exhibit the sharpest curation skills, she still finished her assignment and met its requirements by employing unapproved techniques? Is there any significance to the comparatively smooth and disciplined manner in which Anne completed her pre-curated assignment? The larger question here is what is really being valued and what is being evaluated. Is it the ability to complete an assignment using tools of digital technology? Is it the ability to manoeuvre through vast resources by using critical filtering skills, to identify pertinent information and then utilise it to answer questions, solve diverse and difficult problems, and innovate and create ideas? If so, then that looks something like curation. And to achieve it looks something like digital literacy.

It is also important to explore not just whether or not Sara, Anne, and Paulo were engaged in curation, but how well their digital literacies were recognised and which curation practices could be developed as part of pedagogical improvements. Perhaps this places Anne in a sort of 'Goldilocks zone', where the conditions are conducive for curation to emerge. Another issue that then emerges is if and how we are to enable such conditions for other students and other types of assignments.

Curation as a digital literacy practice has found a home in the personal, educational, and professional lives of students, and this will only grow and become more entrenched over time. When they are well coordinated and used skilfully, they are a natural and seamless addition to research activity and can expand the educational horizon by unlocking access to information. We have seen that, in addition to the skills being taught in each of these courses, the students have skills they have developed from their lives outside the classroom, and each student employed those skills as needed. But we have also seen instances where the students are not sufficiently proficient in the type of critical mindfulness necessary for an educationally viable notion of curation. The skills of curation are essential and having the critical thinking skills to apply them is imperative. However, identifying those skills has not always been the top priority when instituting digital media in the classroom, and if fervent efforts are not made to identify and properly understand curation practices, evaluating and rewarding them through assessment frameworks is doubtful.

Solving problems through synthesising vast amounts of information, often collaboratively, and engaging in exploratory and problem-solving pursuits (rather than just memorising facts and dates) are key skills in the 21st century information-based economy (Wright *et al.*, 2010). Curation practices as I have discussed them here match this new kind of skill set. This is a palette of new skills which some (e.g. Ahmed, 2015) have described as 'hard to assess' using traditional tools of assessment. I have shown that students may already be curators as part of their everyday Internet experience, as witnessed in their assignment-writing strategies. With the right kind of methodology, teachers and researchers can explore and understand these practices further and harness them to create learning opportunities and academic assessment tasks around them.

One conceivable practice which can make the identification and assessment of content curation easier is the requirement of clear and logical signposting in an assignment. We saw an example of how signposting was used in Anne's assignment, but more generally, visually signposting using a web interface and building a narrative around this can be thought of as analogous to 'showing your work' in a math assignment. The Internet is vast and, for many students, a place to get lost and even misguided. Signposting can be a way to leave a digital breadcrumb trail and can be a training tool to remind students to anticipate where they might find information and what the source of their knowledge is.

The proposal for a curated assignment also addresses the practice of "pseudo-writing" as a latent form of plagiarism (Skaar, 2014). In his work on students' pseudo-writing, Skaar argues that teachers should set "locally-based" assignment tasks which are unique to the context of a particular classroom and the student. Such assignment tasks might hold some promise for the nurturing of thinking skills, inspiring different forms of authorship, and other creative practices. Moreover, how Anne and Paulo addressed their assignments is not greatly dissimilar to what Skaar proposes. But the trade-off is one of pre-curation as a form of task guidance. Because of the element of pre-curation in Anne's and Paulo's cases, they did not face the misguiding force of Google's search algorithm in the same way that Sara did. Though all three conducted web searches, Anne and Paulo were insulated from the algorithm by having more guidance and support when it came to the information required for their tasks. And while Paulo's version of the curated assignment was confined by strict guidelines and guiding policies, Anne's version of her curated assignment is more instructional for the ways it encourages various aspects of content curation, allowing for the influence of subjectivity and introducing ways to identify and evaluate curation skills.

But the problems identified with the use of curated assignments, spotlighted already, cannot be forgotten or glossed over. First, the degree to which political actors and policy directives influence the most micro practices of the classroom have proven striking. This can cause, in some extreme cases, an assemblage with political agencies so entangled with learning, that it limits potential for genuinely 'free' learning. If an assignment is pre-curated and a certain outcome is not only anticipated but also desired, pedagogy is not really evaluating appropriateness, style, originality, novelty, creativity, or even authenticity.

Howsoever this is dealt with, what remains a vital lesson to be learned from this research is that if, in this era of informational abundance, we are to acknowledge and incorporate curation practices as integral parts of educational end products—exams or assignments—then we may have to think beyond the notion of a single student creating an 'authentic' text and more about a certain kind of digital literacy which harnesses the wisdom of networks. This would, however, entail a shift in mind-set from literacies which promote a certain kind of originality and uniqueness in writing, to literacies of curation and the new mode of expression they portend.

Networked Wisdom

At the beginning of this chapter, I identified the conditions of content curation as encompassing: problematising and assessing, applying subjective editorial discretion, aggregating and filtering relevant information, adding value to create a new narrative, and presenting that narrative in an appropriate platform. I then used these criteria throughout my analysis of the case studies. These recently emerged digital curation practices occur not just in the classroom but also have become commonplace in everyday life. Curation is not just about the collation of relevant material, although that is a significant part of it; it is also about recontextualising that material in a way that places the curator as consumer and producer at the same time. It is the value added by the curator's subjectivity that makes curation distinguishable, as long as it is not drowned out by volume. The ability to transform ideas existing as content floating on the Internet into emergent concepts under the authorship of a curator is powerful and positions curators as *stewards* of online content. This positioning is important as it radically changes our relationship with online content, and alongside an educationally viable notion of curation, requires thought and analysis applied though discernment and critical awareness.

Early in this chapter I invoked Rosenbaum's (2011) concept of data management, which distinguished between content creation, content aggregation, and content curation. While I have argued that digital content curation requires both the added value of content creation and the discernment and filtering techniques of content aggregation, Rosenbaum's distinctions are nonetheless useful in investigating the challenges encountered within the curation work of assignments. This is because content aggregation is uniquely challenging. What is seen as an easy task of online search can be quite complex. And the reliance on the Internet search engines is only likely to strengthen further as the pool of information on any given subject expands exponentially.

Since no one can process infinite information, we are reliant on searches to filter it. Since results are algorithmically managed, the results we receive are, in a way, predetermined (or pre-curated). Search algorithms exist as crude representations of a searcher's mind and gather clues from data such as a searcher's past browsing history and preferences as a basis rather than truth or morality. Ultimately, this job in searching belongs to the seeker, and the more content that exists online, the more important this role becomes in curation work. The increasing influence of algorithms raises important issues about the nature of algorithmic power, how online information is retrieved, and accountability. These issues need to be further interrogated in sociological terms (Beer, 2009), and curation as a digital literacy practice is one way of contributing to this expanding conversation in sociology.

In this chapter, I have espoused and theorised the curation practices I observed during assignment writing. I have also connected curation as a digital literacy practice to the goals of education, knowledge production, and criticality. If the most basic or naïve goal of education is to gain knowledge, then in the digital age this is knowledge which may require a high degree of discernment. The goal of teaching becomes not just to impart knowledge but also to nurture discernment. In the goal-oriented glorification of knowledge, discernment may not be sufficiently valued as much as it ought to. Curation is a digital literacy practice which necessitates a higher independence level for students. It can also lead to more self-directed and autonomous learning and, through the vast amounts of information that will be encoutered online, can engender an awareness of discernment. Students can create an enhanced sense of ownership towards their work and thereby be more inclined to invest their time and energy working on their course assignments. How curation can then facilitate learning in an assignment-writing scenario and the added value it brings is significant enough for it to be incorporated into assignment tasks and academic project design. This would, of course, require further detailed empirical research which examines how students select and prioritise their searches; what they select, extract, and discard; and how they integrate findings into their writing. In following their paths as they write, we can get to see where they did not go and thus which choices they made and how they were guided by the various actors involved.

Note

1 This quote has been paraphrased to maintain the anonymity of the tutor. The meaning has been retained as closely as possible.

8 Irruption

> In ordinary everyday behavior, in what sense can we examine a talking unless we bring a hearing along with it into account? Or a writing without a reading? Or a buying without a selling?
>
> —(Dewey & Bentley, 1949: 142)

Disruption

The notion of 'disruptive' innovation proposed by Christensen (1997) is a framework to understand the effects new technologies have on markets and business infrastructures. Christensen (1997) claims (see also Christensen *et al.*, 2011) that a disruptive innovation is a process by which a product or service initiates through simple applications at the lower tiers of a market, where users are not being served well by the market as a whole. The service then moves up the market trajectory as technological trends and better quality service allow the innovation to become more 'mainstream'. The disruption occurs through this process of initial and small-scale innovation, the eventual displacement of established competitors, and then the dislodging of previous innovations which relied on a hitherto dominant technology. What therefore emerges is a new paradigm.

An example is the streaming service Netflix, which began as a rather unappealing alternative to mainstream DVD movie rental services. But as its service improved, along with Internet technologies, it eventually became a market leader and dislodged the services of its competitors and the out-dated technologies that those services relied upon. As novel ways of doing things and new technologies replace older methods of carrying out activities, researchers are led to explore the radical reshaping of society that emerges and the performance of new social practices that disruptive innovations bring.

Following this, 'disruptive pedagogy' looks at the impacts of technologies on education and how new technologies can disrupt traditional institutional structures and learning and teaching procedures. Disruptive pedagogies represent a way to understand how traditional methods and tools of learning and teaching can become dislodged by the incorporation of new

Table 8.1 Digital Disruptors

Disruptor	*Disruptee*
Laptop trolleys	Desktops in the ICT suite
SMART boards	Whiteboards
Smartphones	Laptops
Ubiquitous campus Wi-Fi	Wired desktop connections

technologies and innovative educational practices. Following this theory, we can use a simple table to present some examples of disruptive innovations which have occurred in the college classrooms that I observed in this study of assignment writing.

During fieldwork for this study, I noticed disruptors such as laptop trolleys in classrooms and around the departmental areas. These trolleys contained a bank of laptops usually connected to a charge point and were booked by the teachers for use in lessons. A trolley was particularly visible in the case of Sara (Chapter 3) and was instrumental in altering both the form and the function of her classroom. More broadly, the laptop trolleys had alleviated the burden on rooms designated for computer activities at the college, such as ICT suites, which themselves were once major disruptors. Disruptive pedagogies ultimately attempt to become mainstream within the classroom, until they are replaced by a newer disruption.

The speed of obsolescence of technologies causes us to assess the new and disrupted dynamics of digital learning environments continually. However, while looking at things from a 'disruptor' and 'disruptee' perspective might be useful in the study of markets, it does not tell us about the *practices* of how technologies such as college laptop trolleys get used, misused, or disregarded. Disruptors instigate new practices and, as shall be shown as part of this chapter, these are not always predictive.

In this respect, Haxell (2012), in her PhD thesis on the practices of text counselling, argues that to refer to new technologies as 'disruptive' is a "retrospective . . . and positioned naming" (Haxell, 2012: 242), as the label of disruption is limited to the perspective of "those whose experience is disrupted" (Haxell, 2012). For students who prolifically use digital media for such things as text messaging, social networking, and gaming, their deployment of these practices in education is not at all disruptive, since that is their usual way of doing things. If we take a learner-centred and practices-based perspective, there is no disruption from the students per se. Rather, what occurs is a flow of practices into such arenas that may have, in the past, disallowed them to emerge. This is the concept of *irruption* that I advance in this chapter and describe in more detail.

In focusing on the practices of assignment writing, perhaps I can better discuss irruption by asking: is it the instalment of ICTs which transform learning experiences, through disruption, or is it the *practices* enacted in and through the use of ICTs? In this respect, a notion of digital media as actors that instigate irruption is presented here and is based, in part, on the finding that practices which ordinarily have no place in the classroom can *flow* in through their use. Disruption in learning and teaching occurs when a new technology replaces a previous technology or way of doing things (Christensen *et al.*, 2011). Yet how the disruption occurs and what practices cause it to change the culture of a classroom and its established literacy norms are another thing altogether. Disruption is a way to talk about innovation from the point of view of that which is displaced, whereas irruption highlights the displacing practices.

The Flow of Practices

In this study I have drawn attention to how the assignments were assembled and constructed in and through an entanglement of people and things. The heuristic lens of Literacy Studies further led me to put the practices of the assignments as the locus of inquiry and not an a priori conception of 'digital literacy' or a notion of disruption from an institutional perspective. This is to avoid the tendency to see disruption as a 'positioned naming', as Haxell contends, and instead to see the practices as drawing from their own world(s) and bringing something new into being. In other words, what occurs when Sara, Anne, and Paulo use the Internet connectivity and technologies available to them causes various literacy practices to flow into the spatiotemporal world of their assignment writing.

Related to this is the notion of a 'boundary crossing' (Ivanič & Satchwell, 2007; Satchwell *et al.*, 2013)—a phrase deployed to describe literacy practices which crossover contexts. Boundary crossings provide evidence that learners can be sophisticated users of texts outside of their college (e.g. at home or at work), thereby challenging the assumption that a simple 'lack' of literacy holds them back when judged against the literacy paradigm inside college. The findings of Ivanič and Satchwell, as part of their Literacies of Learning in Further Education project (c.f. Ivanič *et al.*, 2009), showed boundary crossing as one of the interfaces between students' literacy practices in their lives beyond the classroom and institution and the different domains of their lives. They argue that the literacy practices taking place in these other domains are a source of knowledge and can, in and of themselves, be tools to leverage learning and ultimately to transform pedagogies. Crossing, however, is a different metaphor to what I am proposing in this chapter. This is because crossings are not without a subsequent transformation; as practices cross assemblage identities, they are transformed and their original purposes betrayed, like the way a dye bleeds into and permeates a textile. The boundary crossing is always volitional and pre-supposes existing contexts, whereas irruption, as I am presenting it here, makes no assumptions about context.

Instead, irruption is a relational activity between actors. Relations between actors can be looked at through the framework of *purification*, *naturalization*, and *translation* (Latour, 1993; Bowker & Star, 1999). Purification entails the exclusion of all behaviours, practices, etc. which are not valorised in the dominant workings of a network. This can look like the setting of standards for digital literacy and directives to uphold what is 'acceptable use' and 'good practice' for educational technology. Naturalization is the ultimate result of this process, insofar as the object of purification becomes taken for granted and treated as monolithic—i.e. 'black-boxed' (Bowker & Star, 1999). Translation, however, is where "mixtures between entirely new types" (Latour, 1993: 10) are created. Translation further relates to "the negotiations, intrigues, calculations, acts of persuasion and violence thanks to which an actor or force takes . . . authority to speak or act on behalf of another actor or force" (Callon & Latour, 1981: 279). Translation is therefore about mobilising actors in support of other actors, and how these coalesce into stabilised linkages to form a 'network' or assemblage. For example, a password to get logged on to a computer, the keyboard and mouse, letters and numbers, and platforms and interfaces. Each of these actors works together to achieve the desired goal of logging on. This framework is particularly useful for tracing the relational interplay of literacy practices because it allows us to look closely at the practices at play—such as a moment of 'logging on'—with recognition of the background practices which make up that brief moment. A moment of logging on then becomes the concern of a study of literacy practices.

Occurrences where entities connect to *translate* into a network include such things as attempts to transform a curriculum through a deeper understanding of college students' literacy practices (e.g. Ivanič *et al.*, 2009), or shift curricula towards work-based learning and recognition of prior experience as course credit (Fenwick & Edwards, 2010). Here I discuss irruption as the mobilisation of digital literacy practices in the writing of assignments as produced through translating actors. Irruption is about the digital literacy practices which originated from somewhere other than the classroom yet were mobilised, with translating actors, into the event and helped to assemble the somewhat precarious entity of the assignment. To understand irruption, therefore, we have to look at how digital literacy practices were organised and systematised not only as part of the assignments, but ultimately as dynamic elements of something else and coming from somewhere else. If we are to describe some of Sara, Anne, and Paulo's practices during the writing of their assignments as irruption, then we must look at where, when, and how they occurred; who and what was involved; and the crucial and strategic roles they played in the completion of their assignments.

Instances of Irruption

A notable example to begin with is when Sara utilised the social networking of her personal life, instead of the institutionally validated Moodle platform of Abbeydale College, to contact a friend to ask for advice on an assignment-related issue. When asked about her social networking activities, interview data reveal that its use infiltrates the contexts of her home, work, and college spheres. She therefore positions herself in multifaceted ways in the web space: as an autonomous learner searching for information, as a confused student seeking assistance, as a friend asking for a favour, to name a few.

Sara casually flouted the college's acceptable use policy: a document which sets out a long list of do's and don't's for technology, applicable both during class time and when using the college's institutional technologies. As an attempt to align actors into a form of naturalization, the college's policy forbids not only phone use in classrooms but also deems 'social' and 'non-educational' interactions as part of its wide list of unacceptable behaviours. Irruption is about the flow of literacy practices that otherwise have no place in the classroom, just as Sara here, through the affordances of the technologies at hand and their connectivity, circumvented a powerful actor's agency as and when she pleased. The communication Sara initiates is a personal one, ostensibly, but the context and motivation are course related. The classroom literacy event is therefore a multi-layered and unbounded phenomenon with ephemeral infiltrations of Sara's personal digital literacy practices. This aspect of the boundaries of the event are further discussed in Chapter 6.

Another way of looking at irruption in Sara's case is by focussing on what took place in the break between the two lessons of a weekly afternoon block: one being a lecture-like instructional lesson and the other being a writing-focussed lesson which followed. As the laptops became deployed in the second lesson, a marked change of pace and behaviour occurred. The laptops were wheeled in on a trolley (see Chapter 3) where they had been kept, pre-charged, and ready under lock and key. Once the laptops were distributed and opened at the desks, the students simultaneously began plugging in their personal mobile devices and listening to music as they worked. It is important to note that personal devices, especially when they are used in this way, are forbidden by the acceptable use policy of Abbeydale College. In line with 'normal' classroom procedure, this rule was abided by throughout the first, lecture-like, lesson with little or no violations. But when the laptop trolley is wheeled in, and when the second lesson begins, a blind eye is turned to the use of personal devices, listening to music, and other new practices that came with the new arrangement. A host of new digital literacy practices have now irrupted into the scene, and the sociomaterial work (and assemblage) of the assignment as its writing unfolds is radically different in manner to the kind of work which occurred before the interim break. The wheeling in of the laptop trolley seemed to be a symbolic shift in mode, method, and culture. It is an actant which acts as a hub to connect the classroom, and the work carried out within it, to a multitude of other actants that are now able to channel practices which were otherwise unpermitted.

In Paulo's and Anne's cases, digital literacy practices irrupted in slightly different ways. Anne's personal reflections on her own blog ended up constituting a crucial part of her assignment writing. This writing is usually about how she and her students (in the course she teaches) have responded to the use of a particular technology or activity in the classroom as well as general posts about her professional life. Anne's writing practices preceded the assignment and her affiliation to her current course, and yet she extracted content from her previous personal blogs and fed it into her current academic assignment. Much of this was a kind of curation practice (see Chapter 7). Similarly, her use of Twitter became connected to the assignment as she linked her portfolio to her Twitter account. Past and future tweets then became part of the life of the assignment, along with the multitudinous and disparate practices nested within each sub-task (see Chapter 6).

During the writing of Paulo's assignment, we see some instances of irruption which are similar to the practices of Anne and Sara, such as when practices of his outside-college life are mobilised as resources for his assignment. For example, when Paulo saved his work at the end of the lesson, he was told not to email it, but rather to upload the document in the VLE through the formal institutional submission process. Instead, Paulo followed the procedure easiest for him and the one which he knew best: to email it. Notably his use of email was not institutional; it was part of his outside-college practices with digital literacy, but (as with Sara) he relied on it here for an assignment-related purpose. He finally managed to correctly upload and submit the assignment formally, but he backed this up with the additional email submission.

There is also another, slightly different, type of irruption occurring during Paulo's assignment writing. Translation between actors is not always predictable and sometimes technologies do not work as we would like, nor do they always follow the script set for them by their designers. Lessons, for example, are often planned by teachers with set activities and timings for all involved. Examples of things not going as planned during Paulo's assignment writing include (i) when the key to the room was unavailable at the start and a designated person who keeps a key for the room had to be found, (ii) when some students had trouble logging in and required an enrolment key to access the VLE, and (iii) when the Java plugin required to play an online video clip failed to download for some of the students.

The disobedience or intransigence of actors renders further actors to burst into action to maintain the apparent coherence of a formal lesson. In the first two examples, it is ICT support staff who must be mobilised into action to make sure the lesson remains on plan and that activities are occurring as they *should* be. This coherence is held in place by certain actors and their scripted practices: lesson plans, timetables, login procedures, etc. But there is somehow always an expectation that things will never go entirely to plan in a classroom, and when problems occur, delays are caused which ultimately impact on the efficiency of workflow for teacher and students. This kind of loss of instructional time is becoming a commonplace occurrence in colleges and universities because of the diversity of technologies and platforms used in classrooms, and the separate log in procedures often required for each (Herold, 2014). Such logistical challenges have resulted in initiatives such as 'single sign-on' which allows students to login to their preferred platform in order to access their school/college learning activity across various platforms.

In sum, irruption occurred during Sara, Paulo, and Anne's assignment writing in a multitude of ways. Each of the assignments relied on instances of irruption, through practices which were either not institutionally valorised, acceptable, or acknowledged. This highlights the importance of investigating whether learners' vernacular practices, past trajectories, social lives, and attitudes associated with digital literacies do—or do not—transfer effectively into classroom work. Since it is classroom-based digital literacies by which learners are ultimately judged, an imposition of its norms can marginalise and deny literacy practices of everyday experience. Researchers, therefore, have the task of making visible the ethnographic detail of what such local, 'everyday' and vernacular digital literacy practices look like and how they can sometimes be mobilised into classroom events through connectivity and digital media. Some researchers and educationalists in the field of learning technologies have tried to address this issue by allowing—and in some cases encouraging—students to bring their own digital devices into the classroom. This is where irruption becomes even more salient.

Device-Oriented Pedagogies

For practitioners seeking to develop pedagogies which capitalise on the affordances of new technologies, insights into digital literacies and practices of irruption in classrooms can support a greater consideration towards how learners experience digital media across different contexts of their lives. Allowing learners' everyday digital literacy practices to be mobilised as resources, either explicitly by them or encouraged and guided by pedagogical approaches, can be supportive to learning. And failure to consider this can widen the gulf between curricular practices and personal digital literacies and their cultures of use.

Irruption, therefore, speaks to debates about digital literacy practices and their contested and controversial place in curricula and everyday lives. Irruption, as advanced here, is about exploring the multi-layered and messy entanglement of social and material actors, and the contested digital literacy practices which ensue as writing unfolds in classrooms during important educational tasks. In this respect, irruption also informs the growing conversation on 'BYOD' (Bring Your Own Device) programmes and strategies in classrooms (e.g. JISC, 2012; Bowman, 2013; Higher Education Academy, 2014).

BYOD is relevant here because it refers to the practice of students' bringing their personally owned digital media devices (usually smartphones or tablets) to classrooms for utilisation during class time, using institutional connectivity and for educational purposes (i.e. academic work). With institutional drives for greater ICT investment and incorporation and the increased costs this brings, BYOD seems for many a convenient 'student-centred' response to the cost-incurring problem of educational technology, given the already pervasive use of devices.

A BYOD project implemented as part of a JISC[1] case study (2014) at the North East Scotland College in November 2013 revealed that students' bringing their own devices is not so straightforward. The study revealed that college Wi-Fi capacity was stretched, ICT administrative systems were not able to sufficiently address learner help requests, electrical safety testing was required on non-institutional devices, and a host of new sockets needed to be installed all over the campus for ease of device charging. Whilst there were some positive effects from the initiative, a host of infrastructural changes and the mobilisations of new actors (sockets, cables, software, technical staff, training courses, etc.) were necessary to implement and manage the BYOD initiative smoothly. Taking practices of irruption into account is a way of gaining insight into the displacing effects such BYOD initiatives have in colleges.

According to the 'Survey of Technology Enhanced Learning for higher education in the UK' by the Universities and Colleges Information Systems Association (Walker *et al.*, 2014), BYOD poses a leading challenge for the future in managing how institutions enable opportunities for learning and providing technical support for staff. As conversations in the field of educational technology gather pace, and yet remain unresolved concerning the role of devices in classrooms, the findings here carry implications for educational practice at all levels where students are prone to device-induced distractions in the classroom. BYOD remains a technology-centred perspective, and this study of the practices of assignment writing shows that bringing one's 'own device' is a catalyst to allow digital literacy practices to irrupt and flow into the conventional learning space—practices which are ordinarily unwelcome or unacknowledged in that space.

Dislodging Conventional Literacies

In this chapter, I have framed some of the notable digital literacy practices which occur during assignment writing as irruption, and explored the role these practices played in both assignment content development and in reshaping, and in some cases dislodging, conventional classroom literacies. I have done this in order to attempt to resolve the divergent approaches surrounding user practices which are commonly applied within the field of learning technologies and its cognate disciplines. As stated at the start of the chapter and also at the end of Chapter 2, the field of learning technologies (and cognate fields) have usually theorised learning through the use of technologies and not through the wider and less predictable construction of user practice—including literate practice—around learning and technology.

Irruption helps us to understand how learners gain pedagogic benefit from digitally mediated forms of communication in educational tasks, including through BYOD. It therefore goes some way to reconcile the "uneasy" (Gourlay *et al.*, 2014: 6) relationship between Literacy Studies and research into learning technologies. Since discovering how learners freely generate learning opportunities through their own digital literacy practices, this kind of inquiry can contribute to a fruitful discussion between disciplinary areas concerned with literacy and learning in digitally mediated environments.

But the argument remains that if educational institutions attempt pedagogical approaches inspired by technological popularity, then a reasonable idea of what students are experiencing with digital media is essential. Strategic visions, good practice initiatives, and acceptable use policies are mere abstractions of interest which position 'disruption' from the vantage point of senior management or from an institutionally established way of doing digital literacy. Explorations of practices of digital literacy which then manage to irrupt into traditional educational spaces can give researchers an indication of the current, creative, and sophisticated practices of digital media which students are able to mobilise, often without solicitation, into a domain to which they may otherwise be unwelcome.

A notion of irruption as I present it here draws attention to how assignments can be done in a multitude of ways, with digital literacy practices emerging in an event and mobilised as resources via the connectivity of cyberspace. The key point is that many of the digital literacy practices which irrupted into the assignments did not cohere with the kinds of literacy practices that Sara, Anne, and Paulo were expected—and directed—to employ. In this way, disruption, as described at the start, is a technology-focussed and perspectival descriptor, whereas irruption is to emphasise the practices which emerge in and through the technology. Irruption is about the digital literacy practices which originated from somewhere other than the classroom (friendship groups, families, work documents, etc.), yet they were mobilised into the event of the classroom and assembled the precarious entity of the assignment. And it is a precarious entity precisely because it required practices from unforeseeable places in order to become successfully completed. To understand assignment writing, therefore, we have to examine empirically how literacy practices are organised and systematised as part of writing and how they gain their meaning and function as dynamic elements of something else.

Note

1 The Joint Information Systems Committee is a UK-based expert body for digital technology and digital resources in education and research.

9 Conclusion

> If literacy is not a given, it remains to be discovered.
>
> (Baynham, 1995: 265)

It is hard to tell a story with a plot that is ever shifting. It is harder still when the setting—its place and time—is also transient. And it is even more so when the actors' relations with each other are symbiotic. That is to say, each actor has something to gain and something to lose in its relation with another actor. But that is the nature of classroom literacy activities and also the nature of this story of assignment writing.

In carrying out this research, I sought to uncover how course assignments were written in college classrooms and how the digital literacy practices of students—emerging whilst they completed their assignments—interacted with the digital demands and requirements of a normative college and classroom environment. In addressing this problem, issues of the shifting and interrelated nature of the assignment narrative were exposed. It then became evident how interrelated my two objectives were. I began to ponder if an assignment-writing event, as a unit of analysis, begins when the task is assigned and ends when it is handed in. The short answer is that it does not. Rather, it is influenced by the history and politics of distant actors, and it also perpetuates into a future where it will be evaluated, appropriated, and recreated into something else—such as a student's results transcript, a spreadsheet (for administrative purposes), or a quality assurance report, for example. We can say, therefore, that the assignment is theoretically timeless; its past and future are encoded within its present. It draws from a multitude of literacy events in its completion, but becomes encased by other literacy events over time.

To speak of an assignment can therefore be to speak of two things: the assignment as performed 'task' and the assignment as 'outcome'. This research speaks to both of these constructs. While it has been chiefly concerned with an assignment as a performance that is maintained for the achievement of predetermined educational goals, it also contributes to a discussion of learning outcomes and standards. Despite my emphasis on the close-up practices of assignment writing, this research also opens a door to issues of educational policy and the role of exogenous actors in classroom practice and educational writing tasks. In carrying out this research, I have also presented a methodology for how writing and literacy can be researched and analysed. This methodological aspect is discussed in detail in my related work (see Bhatt *et al.*, 2015; de Roock *et al.*, 2015; Bhatt, 2017).

To understand the experience of students in a course, and what happens when they are faced with an assignment task, I began this book by using the metaphor of a river to capture the fluid, shifting, and interrelated nature of the practices of assignment writing. Returning to that metaphor, we can view the classroom as a site consisting of many different kinds of boundaries and streams of practices. Boundaries are enacted through such things as walls, locks on doors, password-protected web pages, identity cards (for students, staff, and visitors), and timetables to determine where people should be at any given time in the day-to-day workings of a college. Each of these boundaries serves to separate people of a particular class, course, and college from people in another. There is, therefore, an ostensible distance between them which sometimes must be bridged or overcome. But there are also streams of practices which connect students to places far beyond the classroom, their particular course, and the college in which they reside. My exploration of assignment writing has been about following some of these streams, where they cross with other streams of practices (such as those of teachers and friendship groups) and where they do not. In retrospect, I do not consider myself as having entered the research sites at the start of Sara, Anne, and Paulo's assignments, meaning when their writing began. Instead, I had actually entered existing streams of practices.

Through this research, I have revealed the diverse and boundless practices each student brought to completing his or her work. Each time Sara, Anne, and Paulo employed a 'transgressive' practice, it shifted the plot away from the work of the other, more central actors of assignment completion. These central actors include such things as college policies on digital media use, software scripts, quality inspection reports (themselves morphed into 'action plans' for teachers), and classical notions of literacy. They collectively exert a structuring agency on the kinds of practices that *should* be adopted in the classrooms where they are applied. Furthermore, these actors attempt to standardise assignment writing for every student in a particular course, every year that the course is carried out, and in every college in which that course is provided. They determine a sort of *dramaturgy* of formal learning. Their effects span any particular person, place, or time, and ultimately define and delimit what 'good practice' entails during classroom writing. However, my recording of the assignments using videographic methods, augmented by focussed interviews and observations of institutional digital cultures, exposed more complex relationships. I was led to examine the interplay of those dominant actors against the often hidden and unconventional practices employed by the students of my research and the interdependent relationship between the two.

This interplay was not without a sort of jostling, occasional impasses, and eventually (in some cases) breakthroughs, as some practices hailed from domains that ought not to have been brought into contact with each other, at least according to a conception of digital literacy which was endorsed and upheld by the colleges. The assignments were achieved and written into their final and desired form through the relations between these many actors and their alliances. The students at times appeared to know what was required of them and sometimes acquiesced to procedural norms in their digital literacy practices, but at other times, they were disloyal to them and circumvented policies when they needed or wanted to. This was for the purpose of assignment completion rather than 'fun'. These practices were not exclusively 'personal' in nature, and to label them as such would get in the way of how I have tried to theorise them.

Building upon prior work on practices of the classroom, in Chapter 2, I discussed how the 'Literacies for Learning in Further Education' project drew attention to how curricular practices could be fashioned more around what learners actually bring as resources to classrooms, particularly their digital literacy practices. This is important because the ways that learners embrace a suite of classroom technology is not always reflected in the intentions of the ICT implementers and policymakers who often invoke the logic of 'digital divide' in order to spread digital literacy to the recipients of their investments. I have, therefore, argued that digital literacy is not understood as something which is evaluated exclusively within instructional frameworks. Detailed examinations of students' practices with technology, as investigated in this book, show that students are doing much more with technologies in the classroom, and during assignment tasks, than is intended or conventionally understood.

In this book, I have conceptualised the digital literacy practices of Sara, Anne, and Paulo as 'buried' deep within their set tasks (Chapter 6), like matryushka dolls within moments of literacy. This conception then forces us to slow down, unpack, and trace where practices of digital literacy come from and discover what gives them their specific characteristics. Each moment is a story of practices which emerges through actors that are sometimes behind the scenes in the complex assemblage of assignment writing. Each instruction and activity in the writing process is fraught with choices, dilemmas, and actors which sometimes do not work together effectively. They can be said to include the educational management of the college, the education system, the state, and so on. As we examine the practices and follow the actors, what we see are tasks nested within tasks. And if we look to the future, we will see the assignment emerging in other representations: awarded certificates, data spreadsheets, etc. As an event, the assignment thereby becomes encased by other dolls over time.

Following this, in Chapter 7, I used the term 'curation' to broaden the discussion to knowledge creation practices in assignment writing and how these relate to the skills of discernment while manoeuvring through online content. This investigation into assignment writing revealed two critical discoveries related to curation. First, there is evidence of a degree of what I have called *pre-curation* in classroom assignment tasks. This is when certain actors guide the assignment writing along a certain path and place boundaries around the task to regulate its outcome. Actors which pre-curate in this way can be explicit such as lesson plans, resources lists, and handouts. But they can also be those that are less easy to follow and critique, such as algorithms and sponsored links in search results. It is only when students add their own impressionistic additions, through such things as discernment of content, that the assignment is considered truly curated in the way I have defined it. This is the basis of the second critical discovery on curation.

Curation, as defined in this book, is employed in assignment tasks when students are required to problematise a topic, aggregate relevant information, process that information, contribute to a new narrative around it, and present it in an assigned way. As students engage in this kind of curation, while also being subject to pre-curation, then much of their digital literacy emerges as practices of meaning-making, information management, and knowledge creation. I further argue that curation is a latent form of digital literacy which should be sufficiently acknowledged in education and can even be part of the evaluation and design of assignment tasks as part of an evolving notion of 21st-century skills. This is because digital curation, as part of writing and knowledge creation, necessitates discernment of online content and critical thinking.

In Chapter 8, I respecified the term 'disruption', with its emphasis on organisational change, to what I have defined as 'irruption'. The notion of irruption as I presented it draws attention to the multitude of ways in which assignments can be written. The key point with irruption is that some of the digital literacy practices that emerged in the writing of the assignments were not commensurate with the kinds of literacies that Sara, Anne, and Paulo were expected—and directed—to employ in their assignment work and within the classroom more generally. Irruption attains its significance through its emphasis upon the practices which emerge in, and through, the use of digital media and which thereby dislodge conventional classroom literacies. This is contrasted with disruption, which is a technology-focussed and perspectival descriptor to the deployment of digital media. Talking about irruption, however, allows us to better appreciate and understand the social consequences and effects that technologies have in education.

New approaches to education have been brought about by such things as increased digitisation across society, the need to cater to changing student demographics, and a newly lauded 21st-century skill set. What it means to be digitally literate and what this portends for educational practice is ever shifting. Therefore, the ways in which we practice and think about digital literacies must also be amenable to change. Through this book, I have shown that focusing a lens on student practices as the locus of inquiry allows us to see and value the innovation that students exhibit as they manoeuvre through complex tasks that they have been assigned and how they can ultimately reimagine knowledge through their digital literacies.

Overall, in this book, in light of the cases studied and subsequent analytical discussion in Chapters 6 to 8, what emerges is that the practices I observed were so diverse and unspecific that it becomes inappropriate to pin them down to a set of 'key' skills to be understood and applied the same everywhere. Of course, digital literacy frameworks and taxonomies that elucidate skills and attributes are still important for literacy teachers and educationalists, but what I have shown is that these ought to be based on a detailed explication of localised practices rather than an a priori and managerialist notion of 'what works'. In this way, the implications of this research, and some of the insights gained through its findings, contribute to analytic themes in fields of research beyond Literacy Studies and writing. In particular, I am referring to the fields of educational technology and research into digitised and networked pedagogies.

As the number of studies in these related fields burgeons, new methods of research, new forms of data analysis, and expanded theoretical analyses are provoked as part of a developing sociology of the digital (Edwards *et al.*, 2013). Building on these various inquiries, and particularly those which have emerged in the field of Literacy Studies, let me emphasise at the close of this book what I did at the beginning: This research applies an investigative approach to the study of digital literacies in education. This is one in which digital literacy is not a given and therefore needs to be discovered, and which examines digital literacies as they unfold at the level of practice. This then means that an effective way to understand digital literacies better is through ongoing and wide-ranging research which engages with the users of digital media in specific contexts (schoolchildren, university students, etc.). The aim is not only to gain insights into the range of practices and behaviours with digital media but also to learn how these practices relate to how technologies are positioned by users, teachers, and investors in educational contexts. This would also include designers and engineers in the technology industries. Such inquiry will tell us something about how digital technologies are *supposed* to be used, who ultimately benefits from this positioning in the production of knowledge, and what this portends for knowledge creation as a process.

References

Ahmed, A. (2015) *Assessing 'hard to assess' skills (The future of assessment: 2025 and beyond)*. AQA, [cited 10th October 2015] Available from http://www.aqa.org.uk/about-us/supporting-education/policy/the-future-of-assessment-2025-and-beyond/assessing-hard-to-assess-skills.

Althusser, L. (1977) *Lenin and philosophy and other essays*, New Left Books, London.

Antonio, A., Martin, N. & Stagg, A. (2012) Engaging higher education students via digital curation, In: *Proceedings of the 29th Annual Conference of the Australasian Society for Computers in Learning in Tertiary Education (ASCILITE 2012)*, Wellington: Australasian Society for Computers in Learning in Tertiary Education (ASCILITE), pp. 1–5.

Barthes, R. & Heath, S. (1977) *Image, music, text*, Fontana, London.

Barton, D. (2007) *Literacy: an introduction to the ecology of written language*, Blackwell, Oxford.

Barton, D. & Hamilton, M. (2000) 'Literacy practices', in *Situated literacies: reading and writing in context*, Barton, D., Hamilton, M. & Ivanič, R. (Eds.), Routledge, London, pp. 7–15.

Bawden, D. (2008) 'Origins and concepts of digital literacy', in *Digital literacies: concepts, policies and practices*, Lankshear, C. & Knobel, M. (Eds.), Peter Lang, Oxford, pp. 17–32.

Bayne, S. (2015) 'What's the matter with "technology-enhanced learning"?' *Learning, Media and Technology*, vol. 40, no. 1, pp. 5–20.

Baynham, M. (1995) *Literacy practices: investigating literacy in social contexts*, Longman, London; New York.

Baynham, M. (2004) 'Ethnographies of literacy: introduction', *Language and Education*, vol. 18, no. 4, pp. 285–290.

Baynham, M. & Prinsloo, M. (2001) 'New directions in literacy research', *Language and Education*, vol. 15, no. 2–3, pp. 83–91.

Baynham, M. & Prinsloo, M. (2009) 'Introduction', in *The future of literacy studies*, Baynham, M. & Prinsloo, M. (Eds.), Palgrave Macmillan, Basingstoke, pp. 1–20.

Bazerman, C. (1988) *Shaping written knowledge: the genre and activity of the experimental article in science*, University of Wisconsin Press, Madison, WI.

Bazerman, C. (2010) *Traditions of writing research*, Routledge, New York.

Bazerman, C. & Russell, D. (1994) *Landmark essays on writing across the curriculum*, Hermagoras, Davis, CA.

Beer, D. (2009) 'Power through the algorithm? Participatory web cultures and the technological unconscious', *New Media & Society*, vol. 11, no. 6, pp. 985–1002.

Beetham, H., McGill, L. & Littlejohn, A. (2009) *Thriving in the 21st century: learning literacies for the digital age (LLiDA project)*. London, JISC.

Belshaw, D. (2014) Re*thinking literacy for the web*. EML, [cited 20th April 2014] Available from http://modernlearners.com/rethinking-literacy-for-the-web/.

Besnier, N. (1995) *Literacy, emotion, and authority: reading and writing on a Polynesian atoll*, Cambridge University Press, Cambridge.

Bhatt, I. (2014) *A sociomaterial account of assignment writing in further education classrooms* (PhD diss.), School of Education, University of Leeds.

Bhatt, I. (2017) 'Classroom digital literacies as interactional accomplishments', in *Researching new literacies: design, theory, and data in sociocultural investigation*, Knobel, M. & Lankshear, C. (Eds.), Peter Lang, New York.

Bhatt, I. & de Roock, R. (2013) 'Capturing the sociomateriality of digital literacy events', vol. 21, no. 4, DOI: http://dx.doi.org/10.3402/rlt.v21.21281.

Bhatt, I., de Roock, R. & Adams, J. (2015) 'Diving deep into digital literacy: emerging methods for research', *Language and Education*, vol. 29, no. 6, pp. 477–492.

Bonk, C. J. & Graham, C. R. (2006) *The handbook of blended learning: global perspectives, local designs*, Pfeiffer; [Chichester: John Wiley, distributor], San Francisco.

Bourdieu, P. (1977) *Outline of a theory of practice. (Esquisse d'une théorie de la pratique)*. Translated by Richard Nice. (Repr.), Cambridge University Press, Cambridge.

Bowker, G. C. & Star, S. L. (1999) *Sorting things out: classification and its consequences*, MIT Press, Cambridge, MA; London.

Bowman, S. A. (2013) 'BYOD! We don't think so', in *M-libraries 4: from margin to mainstream—mobile technologies transforming lives and libraries*, Ally, M. & Needham, G. (Eds.), Facet Publishing, London, pp. 47–51.

Brandt, D. & Clinton, K. (2002) 'Limits of the local: expanding perspectives on literacy as a social practice', *Journal of Literacy Research*, vol. 34, no. 3, pp. 337–356.

Brin, S. & Page, L. (2012) 'Reprint of: the anatomy of a large-scale hypertextual web search engine', *Computer Networks*, vol. 56, no. 18, pp. 3825–3833.

Buckingham, D. (2003) *Media education: literacy, learning and contemporary culture*, Polity, Cambridge.

Callon, M. (1986) 'The sociology of an actor-network', in *Mapping the dynamics of science and technology: sociology of science in the real world*, Callon, M., Law, J. & Rip, A. (Eds.), Palgrave Macmillan, Basingstoke, pp. 19–34.

Callon, M. & Latour, B. (1981) 'Unscrewing the big Leviathan: how actors macro-structure reality and how sociologists help them to do so', in *Advances in social theory and methodology: towards an integration of micro- and macro-sociologies*, Knorr-Cetina, K. D. & Cicourel, A. V. (Eds.), Routledge & Kegan Paul, Boston, pp. 277–303.

Chase, Z. & Laufenberg, D. (2011) 'Embracing the squishiness of digital literacy', *Journal of Adolescent & Adult Literacy*, vol. 54, no. 7, pp. 535–537.

Christensen, C. M. (1997) *The innovator's dilemma: when new technologies cause great firms to fail*, Harvard Business School Press, Boston.

Christensen, C. M., Horn, M. B. & Johnson, C. W. (2011) *Disrupting class: how disruptive innovation will change the way the world learns*, McGraw-Hill Professional, New York; London.

Clarke, J. (2002) 'A new kind of symmetry: actor-network theories and the new literacy studies', *Studies in the Education of Adults*, vol. 34, no. 2, pp. 107–122.

Clarke, J. (2008) 'Assembling "skills for life": actor-network theory and the new literacy studies', in *Literacies, global and local*, Prinsloo, M. & Baynham, M. (Eds.), John Benjamins, Amsterdam; Philadelphia, pp. 151–169.

Coiro, J., Knobel, M., Lankshear, C. & Leu, D. J. (2008) *Handbook of research on new literacies*, Taylor & Francis, New York.

Curzon, L. B. (2004) *Teaching in further education: an outline of principles and practice*, Continuum, London.

de Roock, R., Bhatt, I. & Adams, J. (2015) 'Video analysis in digital literacy studies: exploring innovative methods', in *Digital methods for social sciences: an interdisciplinary guide to research innovation*, Snee, H., Hine, C., Morley, Y., Roberts, S. & Watson, H. (Eds.), Palgrave Macmillan, Hampshire, pp. 105–121.

Deleuze, G. & Guattari, F. (1987) *A thousand plateaus: capitalism and schizophrenia*, University of Minnesota Press, Minneapolis.

Deleuze, G. & Guattari, F. (2004) *A thousand plateaus: capitalism and schizophrenia*, Continuum, London.

Dewey, J. & Bentley, A. F. (1949) *Knowing and the known*, Beacon Press, Boston.

Dourish, P. & Button, G. (1998) 'On "Technomethodology": foundational relationships between ethnomethodology and system design', *Human—Computer Interaction*, vol. 13, no. 4, pp. 395–432.

Edwards, A., Housley, W., Williams, M. L. & Sloan, L (2013). 'Digital social research, social media and the sociological imagination: surrogacy, augmentation and re-orientation', *Computational social science: research, design and methods [special issue]. International Journal of Social Research Methodology*, vol. 16, no. 3, pp. 245–260

Edwards, R. (2009) 'Introduction: life as a learning context?', in *Rethinking contexts for learning and teaching*, Edwards, R., Biesta, G. & Thorpe, M. (Eds.), Routledge, London, pp. 1–13.

Edwards, R., Biesta, G. & Thorpe, M. (2009) *Rethinking contexts for learning and teaching*, Routledge, London.

Edwards, R. & Fenwick, T. (2014) 'Critique and politics: a sociomaterialist intervention', *Educational Philosophy and Theory*, vol. 47, no. 13/14, pp. 1385–1404.

Edwards, R., Ivanič, R. & Mannion, G. (2009) 'The scrumpled geography of literacies for learning', *Discourse: Studies in the Cultural Politics of Education*, vol. 30, no. 4, pp. 483–499.

Edwards, R. & Usher, R. (2008) *Globalisation and pedagogy: space, place and identity*, Routledge, London.

Emmel, N. (2008) *Participatory mapping: an innovative sociological method*. Real Life Methods, ESRC, National Centre for Social Research, [cited 1st July 2013] Available from http://eprints.ncrm.ac.uk/540.

English, F. (2011) *Student writing and genre: reconfiguring academic knowledge*, Continuum, London.

Fenwick, T. J. & Edwards, R. (2010) *Actor-network theory in education*, Routledge, London.

Fenwick, T. J. & Edwards, R. (2012) *Researching education through actor-network theory*, John Wiley & Sons, Malden, MA.

Fenwick, T. J., Edwards, R. & Sawchuk, P. (2011) *Emerging approaches to educational research: tracing the sociomaterial*, Routledge, London.

Fiske, J. (2011) *Reading the popular*, Routledge, London.

Foucault, M., Bertani, M., Fontana, A. & Macey, D. (2003) *"Society must be defended": lectures at the College de France, 1975–1976*, Allen Lane, London.

Foucault, M. & Gordon, C. (1980) *Power/knowledge: selected interviews and other writings, 1972/1977*, Harvester Press, Brighton.

Gee, J. P. (2000) 'The new literacy studies: from "socially situated" to the work of the social', in *Situated literacies: reading and writing in context*, Barton, D., Hamilton, M. & Ivanic, R. (Eds.), Routledge, London, pp. 180–196.

Gee, J. P. (2008) *Social linguistics and literacies: ideology in discourses*, Routledge, London.

Gee, J. P. (2010) *New digital media and learning as an emerging area and "worked examples" as one way forwards*, MIT Press, Cambridge, MA.

Geertz, C. (1973) *The interpretation of cultures: selected essays*, Basic Books, New York.

Ghavifekr, S., Afshari, M., Seger, S. S. & Kalaivani, S. (2013) 'ICT application for administration and management: a conceptual review', *Procedia—Social and Behavioral Sciences*, vol. 103, pp. 1344–1351.

Gibson, W. (2005) *God's little toys: confessions of a cut and paste artist.* Wired, July 2005, 118, [cited 20th May 2016] Available from http://www.wired.com/2005/07/gibson-3/.

Gillen, J. (2009) 'Literacy practices in Schome Park: a virtual literacy ethnography', *Journal of Research in Reading*, vol. 32, no. 1, pp. 57–74.

Gillen, J. (2014) *Digital literacies*, Routledge, Abingdon.

Gillen, J. & Barton, D. (2010) *Digital literacies, a research briefing by the technology enhanced learning phase of the Teaching and Learning Research Programme* (TLRP). london Knowledge Lab, Institute of Education, London.

Gilmore, P. (1986) 'Sub-rosa literacy: peers, play and ownership in literacy acquisition', in *The acquisition of literacy: ethnographic perspectives*, Schieffelin, B. B. & Gilmore, P. (Eds.), Ablex, Norwood, NJ, pp. 155–168.

Gilster, P. (1997) *Digital literacy*, John Wiley, Chichester.

Goffman, E. (1961) *Asylums: essays on the social situation of mental patients and other inmates*, Doubleday, Garden City, NY.

Goffman, E. (1990) *The presentation of self in everyday life*, Penguin, London.

Goodfellow, R. & Lea, M. (2013) *Literacy in the digital university: critical perspectives on learning, scholarship & technology*, Routledge, London.

Goody, J. (1977) *The domestication of the savage mind*, Cambridge University Press, Cambridge.

Goody, J. & Watt, I. (1968) 'The consequences of literacy', in *Literacy in traditional societies*, Goody, J. E. (Ed.), Cambridge University Press, Cambridge, pp. 27–68.

Gourlay, L., Hamilton, M. & Lea, M. R. (2014) 'Textual practices in the new media digital landscape: messing with digital literacies', *Research in Learning Technology*, vol. 21, no. 4.

Gourlay, L. & Oliver, M. (2013) 'Beyond "the social": digital literacies as sociomaterial practice', in *Literacy in the digital university: critical perspectives on learning, scholarship & technology*, Goodfellow, R. & Lea, M. (Eds.), Routledge, London, pp. 79–94.

Gunkel, D. J. (2016) *Of remixology: ethics and aesthetics after remix*, MIT Press, Cambridge, MA.

Hamilton, M. (2001) 'Privileged literacies: policy, institutional process and the life of the IALS', *Language and Education*, vol. 15, no. 2/3, pp. 178–196.

Hamilton, M. (2009) 'Putting words in their mouths: the alignment of identities with system goals through the use of individual learning lans', *British Educational Research Journal*, vol. 35, no. 2, pp. 221–242.

Hamilton, M. (2011) 'Unruly practices: what a sociology of translations can offer to educational policy analysis', *Educational Philosophy and Theory*, vol. 43, pp. 55–75.

Havelock, E. A. (1963) *Preface to Plato, Belknap, 1982*, Belknap Press, Cambridge, MA; London.

Havelock, E. A. (1982) *The literate revolution in Greece and its cultural consequences*, Princeton University Press, Princeton; Guildford.

Haxell, A. (2012) *Enactments of change: becoming textually active at Youthline NZ* (PhD thesis), Deakin University.

Hayles, K. (1999) *How we became posthuman: virtual bodies in cybernetics, literature, and informatics*, University of Chicago Press, Chicago; London.

Hayles, K. (2012) *How we think: digital media and contemporary technogenesis*, University of Chicago Press, London.

Heath, S. B. (1982) 'What no bedtime story means: narrative skills at home and school', *Language in Society*, vol. 11, no. 1, pp. 49–76.

Heath, S. B. (1983) *Ways with words: language, life, and work in communities and classrooms*, Cambridge University Press, Cambridge.

Hedberg, J. G. (2006) Searching for disruptive pedagogies: matching pedagogies to the technologies, In: *Keynote address at the Curriculum Corporation 13th National Conference*, Adelaide, Australia.

Hedberg, J. G. (2011) 'Towards a disruptive pedagogy: changing classroom practice with technologies and digital content', *Educational Media International*, vol. 48, no. 1, pp. 1–16.

Herold, B. (2014) 'Software use fuels student-login chaos', *Education Week*, vol. 33, no. 33, pp. 1–16.

Higher Education Academy. (2014) *Mobile learning and Bring Your Own Device (BYOD): gaining better use from familiar technologies and those already owned by students*, [cited 9th May 2014] Available from http://www.heacademy.ac.uk/assets/documents/CLL/Programme_BYOD_7_3_14.pdf.

Hillier, J. (2007) *Stretching beyond the horizon: a multiplanar theory of spatial planning and governance,* Ashgate, Aldershot.

Holme, R. (2004) *Literacy: an introduction*, Edinburgh University Press, Edinburgh.

Hutchins, E. (1995) *Cognition in the wild*, MIT Press, Cambridge, MA; London.

Ivanič, R. (2009) 'Bringing literacy studies into research on learning across the curriculum', in *The future of literacy studies*, Baynham, M. & Prinsloo, M. (Eds.), Palgrave Macmillan, Basingstoke, pp. 100–122.

Ivanič, R., Edwards, R., Barton, D., Martin-Jones, M., Fowler, Z., Hughes, B., Mannion, G., Miller, K., Satchwell, C. & Smith, J. (2009) *Improving learning in college: rethinking literacies across the curriculum*, Routledge, London.

Ivanič, R. & Satchwell, C. (2007) 'Boundary crossing: networking and transforming literacies in research processes and college courses', *Journal of Applied Linguistics*, vol. 4, no. 1, pp. 101–124.

James, W. (1907) *Pragmatism, a new name for some old ways of thinking: popular lectures on philosophy*, Harvard University Press, Cambridge, MA.

JISC. (2012) *Bring Your Own Device (BYOD)*, [cited 9th May 2014] Available from http://www.jisc.ac.uk/blog/bring-your-own-device-byod-23-nov-2012.

JISC. (2014) *Bring Your Own Device (BYOD)—One college's journey*. JISC RSC Scotland iTech Case Study. Available from http://www.rsc-scotland.org/wp-content/uploads/2014/05/20140124NorthEastScotland.pdf.

Jones, C. (2015) *Networked learning: an educational paradigm for the age of digital networks*, Springer, London.

Jowett, B. (2008) *The Phædrus of Plato*. Translated by Benjamin Jowett, Forgotten Books, Charleston, SC.

Kell, C. (2006) 'Crossing the margins: literacy, semiotics and the recontextualisation of meanings', in *Travel notes from the new literacy studies: instances of practice*, Pahl, K. & Rowsell, J. (Eds.), Multilingual Matters, Clevedon, pp. 147–171.

Kell, C. (2009) 'Literacy practices, text/s and meaning making across time and space', in *The future of literacy studies*, Baynham, M. & Prinsloo, M. (Eds.), Palgrave Macmillan, Basingstoke, pp. 75–99.

Knobel, M. & Lankshear, C. (2008) 'Remix: the art and craft of endless hybridization', *Journal of Adolescent & Adult Literacy*, vol. 52, no. 1, pp. 22–33.

Kwa, C. (2002) 'Romantic and baroque conceptions of complex wholes in the sciences', in *Complexities: social studies of knowledge practices,* Law, J. & Mol, A. (Eds.), Duke University Press, Durham; London, pp. 23–52.

Lankshear, C. & Knobel, M. (2011) *New literacies: everyday practices and social learning: everyday practices and social learning*, McGraw-Hill Education, New York.

Latour, B. (1987) *Science in action: how to follow scientists and engineers through society*, Open University Press, Milton Keynes.

Latour, B. (1991) 'Technology is society made durable', in *A sociology of monsters: essays on power, technology and domination*, Law, J. (Ed.), Routledge, London, pp. 103–131.

Latour, B. (1993) *We have never been modern*, Harvester Wheatsheaf, New York; London.

Latour, B. (1996) *Aramis: or the love of technology*, Harvard University Press, Cambridge, MA; London.

Latour, B. (1999) 'On recalling ANT', in *Actor-network theory and after*, Law, J. & Hassard, J. (Eds.), Blackwell Publishers, Oxford, pp. 15–26.

Latour, B. (2004) 'Nonhumans', in *Patterned ground: entanglements of nature and culture*, Harrison, S., Pile, S. & Thrift, N. J. (Eds.), Reaktion, London, pp. 224–227.

Latour, B. (2005) *Reassembling the social: an introduction to actor-network-theory*, Oxford University Press, Oxford.

Latour, B. & Woolgar, S. (1986) *Laboratory life: the construction of scientific facts*, Princeton University Press, Princeton.

Latta, R. (1898) *The monadology and other philosophical writings*, Oxford University Press, Oxford.

Law, J. (1999) 'After ANT: Complexity, Naming and Topology', in *Actor-network theory*, Hassard, J. & Law, J. (Eds.), Blackwell,Oxford.

Law, J. (2009) 'Actor network theory and material semiotics', in *The new Blackwell companion to social theory*, Turner, B. S. (Ed.), Wiley-Blackwell, Oxford, pp. 141–158.

Law, J. (2012) 'Collateral realities', in *The politics of knowledge*, Rubio, F. D. & Baert, P. (Eds.), Routledge, London, pp. 156–178.

Law, J. & Hassard, J. (1999) *Actor network theory and after*, Blackwell, Oxford.

Lessig, L. (2008) *Remix: making art and commerce thrive in the hybrid economy*, Bloomsbury Academic, London.

Livingstone, S. (2012) 'Critical reflections on the benefits of ICT in education', *Oxford Review of Education*, vol. 38, no. 1, pp. 9–24.

Luria, A. R. (1976) *Cognitive development: its cultural and social foundations*, Harvard University Press, Cambridge, MA; London.

Martin, A. & Grudziecki, J. (2007) 'DigEuLit: concepts and tools for digital literacy development', *Italics*, vol. 5, no. 4., pp. 1–19.

Marvin, C. (1988) *When old technologies were new: thinking about electric communication in the late nineteenth century*, Oxford University Press, Oxford.

Matthewman, S. D. (2013) 'Michel Foucault, technology, and actor-network theory', *Techné: Research in Philosophy and Technology*, vol. 17, no. 2, pp. 274–292.

Melzer, D. (2009) 'Writing assignments across the curriculum: a national study of college writing', *College Composition and Communication*, vol. 61, no. 2, pp. 240–261.

Miller, D. (2013) *Facebook's so uncool, but it's morphing into a different beast [The Conversation]*, [cited 19th October 2014] Available from http://theconversation.com/facebooks-so-uncool-but-its-morphing-into-a-different-beast-21548.

Mol, A. (1999) 'Ontological politics: a word and some questions', in *Actor network theory and after*, Law, J. & Hassard, J. (Eds.), Blackwell, Oxford, pp. 74–89.

Mol, A. (2002) *The body multiple: ontology in medical practice*, Duke University Press, Durham; London.

Nash, I., Jones, S., Ecclestone, K. & Brown, A. (2008) *Challenge and change in further education: a commentary by the teaching and learning research programme*. TLRP. Available from http://www.tlrp.org/pub/documents/FEcommentary.pdf.

The New Media Consortium. (2005) *A Global Imperative—the report of the 21st century literacy summit*, [cited 12th March 2014] Available from http://www.nmc.org/pdf/Global_Imperative.pdf.

Nicholls, A. V. (2009) *The social life of the computer in ramingining* (PhD thesis), Charles Darwin University.

Norris, P. (2001) *Digital divide? Civic engagement, information poverty, and the Internet worldwide*, Cambridge University Press, Cambridge.

Olson, D. R. (1977) 'From utterance to text: the bias of language in speech and writing', *Harvard Educational Review*, vol. 47, no. 3, pp. 257–281.

Ong, W. J. (1982) *Orality and literacy: the technologizing of the word*, Routledge, London.

Orlikowski, W. J. (2007) 'Sociomaterial practices: exploring technology at work', *Organization Studies*, vol. 28, no. 9, pp. 1435–1448.

Parry, D. (2011) 'Mobile perspectives: on teaching mobile literacy', *EDUCAUSE Review*, vol. 46, no. 2, pp. 14–16.

Parsons, J. & Clarke, B. (2013) 'Rhizomic thinking: towards a new consideration of social studies practice', *Social Studies Research and Practice*, vol. 8, no. 3, pp. 89–98.

Pecorari, D. (2003) 'Good and original: plagiarism and patchwriting in academic second-language writing', *Journal of Second Language Writing*, vol. 12, no. 4, pp. 317–345.

Pegrum, M. (2010) ' "I link, therefore I am": network literacy as a core digital literacy', *E-Learning and Digital Media*, vol. 7, no. 4, pp. 346–354.

Petersen, S. M. (2007) 'Mundane cyborg practice: material aspects of broadband internet use', *Convergence: The International Journal of Research into New Media Technologies*, vol. 13, no. 1, pp. 79–91.

Prinsloo, M. & Baynham, M. (2008) 'Introduction: renewing literacy studies', in *Literacies, global and local,* Prinsloo, M. & Baynham, M. (Eds.), John Benjamins, Amsterdam; Philadelphia, pp. 1–16.

Rheingold, H. (2010) *Attention, and other 21st-century social media literacies*, [cited 9th May 2014] Available from http://www.educause.edu/ero/article/attention-and-other-21st-century-social-media-literacies.

Rheingold, H. (2012) *Net smart: how to thrive online*, MIT Press, Cambridge, MA; London.

Roberge, M., Siegal, M. & Harklau, L. (2009) *Generation 1.5 in college composition: teaching academic writing to U.S.-educated learners of ESL*, Routledge, London.

Rosenbaum, S. C. (2011) *Curation nation: how to win in a world where consumers are creators*, McGraw-Hill Professional; [London: McGraw-Hill, distributor], New York.

Rowan, L. & Bigum, C. (2012) *Transformative approaches to new technologies and student diversity in futures oriented classrooms: future proofing education*, Springer, Dordrecht; London.

Salmon, G. (2004) *E-moderating: the key to teaching and learning online*, RoutledgeFalmer, London.

Satchwell, C., Barton, D. & Hamilton, M. (2013) 'Crossing boundaries: digital and non-digital literacy practices in formal and informal contexts in further and higher education', in *Literacy in the digital university: critical perspectives on learning, scholarship & technology*, Goodfellow, R. & Lea, M. (Eds.), Routledge, London, pp. 42–55.

Schieffelin, B. B. & Gilmore, P. (1986) *The acquisition of literacy: ethnographic perspectives*, Ablex, Norwood, NJ.

Scollon, R. & Scollon, S. B. K. (1981) *Narrative, literacy, and face in interethnic communication*, Ablex, Norwood, NJ.

Scribner, S. & Cole, M. (1981) *The psychology of literacy*, Harvard University Press, Cambridge, MA.

Simpson, J., Cooke, M. & Baynham, M. (2008) *The right course? An exploratory study of learner placement practices in ESOL and literacy*, National Research and Development Centre for Adult Literacy and Numeracy, London.

Skaar, H. (2014) 'Writing and pseudo-writing from Internet-based sources: implications for learning and assessment', *Literacy*, vol. 49, no. 2, pp. 69–76, DOI: 10.1111/lit.12045.

Smith, J. (2005) 'Mobilising everyday literacy practices within the curricula', *Journal of Vocational Education & Training*, vol. 57, no. 3, pp. 319–334.

Smith, J., Satchwell, C., Edwards, R., Miller, K., Fowler, Z., Gaechter, J., Knowles, J., Phillipson, C. & Young, R. (2008) 'Literacy practices in the learning careers of childcare students', *Journal of Vocational Education & Training*, vol. 60, no. 4, pp. 363–375.

Snyder, I. (2002) *Silicon literacies: communication, innovation and education in the electronic age*, Routledge, London.

Snyder, I. (2015) 'Discourses of "curation" in digital times', in *Discourse and digital practices: doing discourse analysis in the digital age*, Jones, R., Chik, A. & Hafner, C. (Eds.), Routledge, Abingdon, pp. 209–225.

Soliday, M. (2011) *Everyday genres: writing assignments across the disciplines*, Southern Illinois University Press; [London: Eurospan, distributor], Carbondale, IL.

Sørensen, E. (2010) *The materiality of learning: technology and knowledge in educational practice*, Cambridge University Press, Cambridge.

Steiner, C. (2012) *Automate this: how algorithms came to rule our world*, Portfolio/Penguin, New York.

Street, B. V. (1984) *Literacy in theory and practice*, Cambridge University Press, Cambridge.

Street, B. V. (1993) *Cross-cultural approaches to literacy*, Cambridge University Press, Cambridge.

Street, B. V. (1995) *Social literacies: critical approaches to literacy in development, ethnography and education*, Longman, London.

Street, B. V. (1997) 'The implications of the "new literacy studies" for literacy Education', *English in Education*, vol. 31, no. 3, pp. 45–59.

Street, B. V. (2009) 'The future of "social literacies"', in *The future of literacy studies*, Baynham, M. & Prinsloo, M. (Eds.), Palgrave Macmillan, Basingstoke, pp. 21–37.

Street, B. V. & Leftsein, A. (2007) *Literacy: an advanced resource book for students*, Routledge, London.

Tufte, E. R. (1990) *Envisioning information*, Graphics Press, Cheshire, CT.

Tusting, K., Ivanič, R. & Wilson, A. (2000) 'New literacy studies at the inter-change', in *Situated literacies*, Barton, D., Hamilton, M. & Ivanič, R. (Eds.), Routledge, London, pp. 210–218.

van Heur, B., Leydesdorff, L. & Wyatt, S. (2013) 'Turning to ontology in STS? Turning to STS through "ontology"', *Social Studies of Science*, vol. 43, no. 3, pp. 341–362.

von Leibniz, G. W. F., Francks, R. & Woolhouse, R. S. (1998) *Philosophical texts*, Oxford University Press, Oxford.

Vrasidas, C. & Glass, G. V. (2005) *Preparing teachers to teach with technology, information age*, Information Age Publishing, [London: Eurospan, distributor], Greenwich, CT.

Walker, R., Voce, J., Nicholls, J., Swift, E., Ahmed, J., Horrigan, S. & Phil, V. (2014) *2014 Survey of technology enhanced learning for higher education in the UK*. UciSA, [cited 20th October 2014] Available from http://www.ucisa.ac.uk/~/media/groups/dsdg/Tel%202014%20Final%2018%20August.ashx.

Waltz, S. B. (2006) 'Nonhumans unbound: actor-network theory and the reconsideration of "Things" in Educational Foundations', *Educational Foundations*, vol. 20, no. 3, pp. 51–68.

Warschauer, M. (1999) *Electronic literacies: language, culture, and power in online education*, Lawrence Erlbaum, Mahwah, NJ.

Weller, M. (2011) *The digital scholar: how technology is transforming scholarly practice*, Bloomsbury Academic, London.

White, N. B. (2012) *Understanding content curation.iInnovations in education*, [cited 6th April 2014] Available from http://d20innovation.d20blogs.org/2012/07/07/understanding-content-curation/.

Wright, J., Brinkley, I. & Clayton, N. (2010) *Employability and skills in the UK: redefining the debate*, Work Foundation, London.

Index

For Product Safety Concerns and Information please contact our EU
representative GPSR@taylorandfrancis.com
Taylor & Francis Verlag GmbH, Kaufingerstraße 24, 80331 München, Germany

www.ingramcontent.com/pod-product-compliance
Ingram Content Group UK Ltd.
Pitfield, Milton Keynes, MK11 3LW, UK
UKHW021958180926
475701UK00003B/85

* 9 7 8 0 3 6 7 1 9 4 2 9 1 *